Money Finally Makes Sense

The No-Jargon, No-Guilt Guide to Managing Your Money and Building Wealth

Alex Z. Morgan

Clear Money Press

Copyright

Published by Clear Money Press. First Edition, 2026.

Disclaimer

This book is for educational purposes only and is not personalized financial, tax, or investment advice. The full notice to readers follows overleaf.

DISCLAIMER

Important Notice to Readers

Not Financial Advice

This book is for educational purposes only and does not constitute personalized financial, tax, or investment advice. Consult a licensed financial professional before making significant financial decisions.

Individual Circumstances Vary

Financial strategies that are appropriate for one person may not be appropriate for another. Your specific situation, tax obligations, and goals should guide your decisions.

Information Currency

Tax laws, contribution limits, and financial regulations change frequently. Verify current limits and rules with official sources (IRS, SEC) before acting on information in this book.

Important Notice to Readers

Table of Contents

INTRODUCTION

Why Personal Finance Feels Harder Than It Is

The personal finance industry profits from your confusion. This book ends that.

Personal finance is not complicated. The core principles that produce financial security and wealth over a lifetime can be explained clearly in a few pages. The actions required to implement those principles are not technically demanding. And yet most people find money stressful, confusing, and anxiety-producing — evidence not that personal finance is inherently difficult, but that it has been presented in ways that serve the financial industry's interests more than the average person's.

Financial institutions, investment platforms, insurance companies, and the personal finance publishing industry all have business incentives to make money management seem complex enough that you need their products, services, and guidance. When money feels confusing and overwhelming, people make worse financial decisions — often decisions that benefit the entities selling them products rather than their own financial futures.

This book is a corrective. It presents the fundamentals of personal finance in plain language, without jargon, without judgment about past decisions, and without trying to sell you anything. The goal is to give you a clear, working understanding of how money works and a practical system for managing it — one that takes less time each month than watching a single television episode.

The secret to wealth is simple: spend less than you earn, invest the surplus, avoid debt. Do this consistently over a lifetime and financial security is almost mathematically inevitable.

One final note before we begin: financial improvement is not linear. You will have months of excellent financial discipline followed by months where life intervenes and progress stalls or reverses. This is normal. The measure of financial success over a lifetime is not the absence of setbacks but the overall direction of the trend line. Consistency over years and decades — not perfection over days and weeks — is what produces financial security and freedom.

Why Most People Struggle Financially

Financial struggle in modern developed economies is rarely caused by insufficient income. Studies consistently show that people at a wide range of income levels — including people who earn more than most — report feeling financially stressed, living paycheck to paycheck, and lacking basic financial security. The cause is not income; it is the absence of a system.

Without a system, financial decisions are made reactively — in response to immediate desires, social pressure, marketing, and circumstances — rather than proactively in alignment with longer-term goals. Without a system, there is no reliable mechanism by which income translates into savings and investment. Without a system, debt accumulates gradually and invisibly until it becomes a significant burden.

This book provides the system. It is not a complicated system. It does not require advanced financial knowledge, significant time investment, or sacrifice of all enjoyment. It requires understanding a small number of key principles and implementing a small number of deliberate practices. Followed consistently, it produces financial results that most people assume require either high income or specialized knowledge.

The Five Core Principles

Every chapter in this book elaborates on one of five core principles of personal finance. Understanding these principles before reading the detailed chapters provides a conceptual framework that makes everything else easier to integrate.

- Principle 1: Spend less than you earn. This is the foundational principle of all personal finance. No strategy works if outflows consistently exceed inflows.
- Principle 2: Pay yourself first. Savings and investments should come out of income before discretionary spending, not from what is left over after spending.
- Principle 3: Time is the most powerful variable in wealth building. Starting to invest earlier, even with small amounts, produces dramatically better outcomes than starting later with larger amounts.
- Principle 4: Avoid bad debt; use good debt carefully. High-interest consumer debt is one of the most powerful destroyers of financial progress. Mortgage debt used sensibly can support wealth building.
- Principle 5: Protect what you build. Insurance, estate planning, and adequate emergency reserves prevent catastrophic financial setbacks that can undo years of progress.

How to Use This Book

Each chapter covers one major domain of personal finance, and most end with an action item — a specific financial task you can complete this week that moves you forward in that domain. The chapters are sequenced in the order that produces the best results: foundation before investing, debt before retirement accounts (with some important exceptions), protection after accumulation.

Read the chapters in order on first pass. Return to individual chapters as reference when you need to make decisions in specific domains. The Appendix provides quick-reference resources you will return to repeatedly over time.

Why Most Personal Finance Advice Fails

Most personal finance advice fails people not because it is technically wrong but because it ignores the human context in which financial decisions are actually made. Generic prescriptions — "spend less than you earn," "invest early and often," "avoid lifestyle inflation" — are correct but not useful, because the people who need them most already know them and still do not follow them. Knowing what to do and being able to do it consistently are separated by the entire domain of behavioral psychology, personal history, emotional patterns, and environmental design.

This book takes a different approach. Each chapter addresses not only what to do but why people struggle to do it, and provides the specific behavioral strategies that make the right actions more sustainable. Understanding why the knowledge-behavior gap exists for each financial domain — and what structural interventions close it — is the knowledge that converts financial information into financial progress.

The Emotional Side of Money

Money decisions are emotional decisions. The evidence is everywhere: people hold losing investments longer than winning ones because of loss aversion, not rational calculation. People spend more when paying by credit card than cash because the payment is temporally separated from the purchase, reducing its psychological impact. People save less than they intend to because the future self who will need retirement income feels like a stranger relative to the present self who wants to spend. These are not character flaws — they are documented patterns of human psychology that affect even financially sophisticated people.

The most financially successful people are not those who have transcended emotion in financial decision-making. They are those who have built financial systems that work with their emotional patterns rather than requiring constant resistance to them. Automated savings that remove money before it can be spent, separate accounts for specific purposes that reduce the cognitive availability of money for other uses, investing rules that prevent emotional selling during market downturns — these structures produce good financial outcomes by aligning with human psychology rather than fighting it.

As you implement the principles in this book, pay attention to the emotional responses that financial decisions generate in you. Anxiety when you check your account balance, avoidance of financial statements, guilt when you spend on something you enjoy, resentment when you follow your budget — these emotional signals contain information about the specific psychological patterns that are shaping your financial behavior. Addressing them is not separate from financial planning; it is financial planning at its most sophisticated level.

CHAPTER 1

Your Money Mindset: The Psychology Behind Financial Decisions

---

Your financial behavior is shaped far more by psychology than by knowledge. Understanding this is where real financial change begins.

> ***"A budget is telling your money where to go instead of wondering where it went." — John Maxwell***

Financial transformation doesn't begin with a spreadsheet. It begins with an honest examination of the beliefs, emotions, and behavioral patterns that have shaped your financial life to date. The most financially sophisticated person with destructive money scripts will consistently underperform the financially less educated person with healthy money beliefs. This chapter is the foundation everything else builds on.

Most personal finance books skip the psychology and jump straight to the numbers — budgets, investment accounts, debt payoff calculators. This is a significant oversight. The reason most people don't implement financially sound advice isn't that they lack information. They can find virtually any financial information they need within minutes online. The reason is that their relationship with money — the emotions, beliefs, and behavioral patterns surrounding financial decisions — actively works against implementation.

Why Financial Education Alone Doesn't Work

The United States has some of the most financially educated consumers in the world, as measured by the volume of personal finance books, media, courses, and educational programs available. It also has some of the most financially stressed households — high consumer debt, low savings rates, and inadequate retirement preparation are widespread at all income levels. This paradox reveals an important truth: knowing what to do financially is not the same as doing it.

The gap between financial knowledge and financial behavior is the central problem that this book addresses. The solution is not more information — it is understanding the psychological mechanisms that drive financial behavior and designing systems that work with those mechanisms rather than relying on willpower and rational analysis to override them. This is why the psychology chapter comes first: everything else in this book builds on the foundation of understanding how financial decisions actually get made.

The Emotional Dimension of Money

Money carries emotional weight that far exceeds its practical function as a medium of exchange. For most people, money is entangled with feelings of security, freedom, self-worth, power, love, and social belonging. Financial decisions are rarely purely rational calculations — they are emotionally laden choices in which the psychological meaning of the transaction often matters more than the financial impact.

This emotional dimension explains behaviors that appear financially irrational: spending money on status items when basic needs are unmet; avoiding looking at bank account balances because the number produces anxiety; lending money to family members even when it creates genuine hardship; delaying retirement savings for years because "retirement feels far away." These are not stupidity or weakness — they are predictable responses to the psychological meaning that money carries.

Money Scripts: The Beliefs Running Your Financial Life

Financial psychologist Brad Klontz developed the concept of money scripts — unconscious beliefs about money absorbed in childhood and early adulthood that drive financial behavior as adults. The four primary money script categories: Money Avoidance (money is bad, rich people are greedy, I don't deserve financial success); Money Worship (money will solve all my problems, more money equals more happiness); Money

Status (my net worth equals my self-worth, I need to appear wealthy); and Money Vigilance (I must always save, spending money is dangerous, I should never discuss money).

Each script produces predictable financial behaviors. Money Avoidance scripts lead to self-sabotage of income and savings. Money Worship scripts lead to perpetual dissatisfaction and overspending in pursuit of more. Money Status scripts lead to lifestyle inflation and social spending that prevents wealth accumulation. Money Vigilance scripts lead to underinvestment and financial anxiety even when circumstances are secure.

Identifying Your Money Script

Reflect on the messages about money you received growing up. What did your parents say — or not say — about money? What behaviors did they model? What beliefs about wealth, spending, and financial status were implicit in your household? These early experiences are the most common source of money scripts, and identifying them is the first step toward updating them.

The Financial Therapy Movement

Financial therapy — the integration of therapeutic techniques with financial planning — has emerged as a recognized discipline over the past decade, reflecting the growing acknowledgment that financial problems are often as much psychological as mathematical. Financial therapists work with clients to identify the emotional roots of financial behaviors: the anxiety that prevents someone from looking at bank statements, the compulsive spending that provides emotional relief, the avoidance of estate planning because it requires contemplating mortality.

You don't need a financial therapist to benefit from financial therapy insights. The most valuable practice is simple reflection: when you notice a financial behavior that seems inconsistent with your stated goals or values, get curious about it rather than critical. Ask: what emotion is this behavior serving? What would I feel if I changed it? What belief about money or myself is underneath this pattern? These questions don't require a therapist — they require only honest self-inquiry.

The Money Dialogue Practice

Write a letter to money as if it were a person. Describe your relationship with it — what you feel, what you want from it, what you fear about it, what you resent about it. This exercise, used by financial therapists, often surfaces money scripts and emotional patterns that rational analysis doesn't reveal. The letter doesn't need to be shared with anyone. Its value is in the writing.

Cognitive Biases in Financial Decision-Making

Beyond money scripts, a set of cognitive biases documented by behavioral economists consistently produce poor financial decisions across populations. Understanding these biases is valuable not because it eliminates them — they are deeply embedded in human cognition — but because naming them helps you recognize when they might be influencing a financial decision.

Present Bias

Present bias is the tendency to overweight immediate rewards relative to future rewards. It is why people consistently choose a smaller immediate payment over a larger future one, and why retirement savings — which require immediate sacrifice for distant reward — feel harder than any equivalent immediate financial obligation. Present bias is the primary psychological force that retirement account design (automatic enrollment, employer matching, pre-tax contributions) attempts to counteract.

Loss Aversion

Research by Kahneman and Tversky showed that the psychological pain of losing $100 is approximately twice as powerful as the psychological pleasure of gaining $100. This asymmetry produces predictable poor financial decisions: holding losing investments longer than optimal because selling would "lock in" a loss; avoiding investing entirely because the prospect of investment loss feels worse than the certainty of slow inflation erosion.

Mental Accounting

Mental accounting is the tendency to treat money differently depending on its source, its intended purpose, or the account in which it is held — even when money is fungible and all of it is equally valuable. Tax refunds are spent more freely than earned income. Casino winnings are gambled more freely than saved income. "Found money" is treated differently than earned money. Recognizing mental accounting prevents the category-specific inconsistencies it produces.

Building a Positive Financial Identity

Just as health behaviors are more sustainable when anchored in identity, financial behaviors benefit enormously from a supportive financial self-concept. Research on financial behavior consistently finds that people who describe themselves as "good with money" — regardless of their current financial situation — make better financial decisions than those who describe themselves as "bad with money." The self-concept becomes a self-fulfilling prophecy.

Building a positive financial identity doesn't require pretending your current situation is better than it is. It requires distinguishing between your current financial circumstances (which are a result of past choices and conditions) and your financial competence (your capacity to make better choices going forward). Your past financial decisions don't define your future financial potential — but your beliefs about your own financial capability will.

The Financial Identity Statement

Write a one-sentence financial identity statement: "I am someone who..." that reflects the financial person you are becoming rather than the one your past behavior suggests. Examples: "I am someone who makes deliberate financial decisions aligned with my values." "I am someone who builds financial security steadily over time." "I am someone who understands money and manages it well." Post this statement where you will see it regularly. The identity reinforcement effect is real.

The Financial Psychology of Scarcity and Abundance

The scarcity mindset — the psychological experience of not having enough — creates cognitive impairment that makes financial decisions worse. Research by Anandi Mani, Sendhil Mullainathan, Eldar Shafir and Jiaying Zhao found that poverty imposes a cognitive tax: the mental bandwidth consumed by financial stress reduced performance on tests of reasoning and impulse control by what the authors calibrated as the equivalent of about 13 IQ points. The size of that effect has been contested since, but the direction — that financial scarcity consumes attention that would otherwise be available for decisions — is well supported. This is not a character flaw of people experiencing financial stress — it is the predictable cognitive effect of operating under resource scarcity.

The abundance mindset — the psychological experience of having enough, even when your current resources are modest — is not about denying financial reality. It is about directing attention toward resources and possibilities rather than deficits and threats. This reorientation has measurable effects on financial decision-making quality. People in an abundance orientation make better long-term financial choices, are more likely to save, and are less susceptible to the impulsive financial decisions that scarcity psychology generates. Building financial systems that reduce the constant salience of resource scarcity — automating savings before you can spend them, creating buffer accounts that prevent account-emptying anxiety — is as much psychological as financial.

Changing Your Financial Story

The narrative you tell about your relationship with money — inherited from family, formed by early financial experiences, reinforced by years of financial behavior — is one of the most powerful determinants of your future financial outcomes. People who tell themselves "I am bad with money" demonstrate a self-fulfilling prophecy: they avoid financial engagement, make financial decisions impulsively, and attribute financial problems to fixed character rather than changeable behavior. People who adopt a learning orientation — "I am developing my financial skills" — respond to financial setbacks as information rather than confirmation of inadequacy.

Changing a deeply held financial story requires both narrative work — deliberately constructing a more accurate story about your relationship with money — and behavioral evidence. The behavioral evidence matters most: each financial decision made according to your values, each savings milestone reached, each debt payment made adds evidence that contradicts the old story and supports the new one. This is the same identity-based behavior change principle that applies to any habit change. You become someone who manages money well by managing money well, repeatedly, until the evidence accumulates.

The Financial Behavior Gap and How to Close It

Financial knowledge and financial behavior are not the same thing. Most people who carry high-interest credit card debt know they should pay it off faster. Most people who have not started saving for retirement know they should. The gap between knowing and doing is the central challenge of personal finance, and it is addressed not through more information but through behavior change strategies.

The most effective strategies for closing the financial behavior gap: make the desired behavior the default through automation, reduce the friction of starting (opening the account today rather than "when I have more time"), and create social accountability (telling a trusted person your financial goal and checking in on progress). These strategies work because they reduce the reliance on motivation and willpower that the behavior gap relies on. A savings transfer that happens automatically does not require daily motivation to execute.

Values Clarification as Financial Foundation

Before any specific financial technique is useful, the question of what you are building toward needs an honest answer. Most people have never clearly articulated what a financially successful life looks like to them — they pursue generic financial goals (retire early, have a million dollars, be debt-free) without connecting them to the specific experiences and freedoms those goals would provide. This disconnection between financial goals and life values is one of the primary reasons people fail to sustain financial effort over the years required to reach significant financial milestones.

Spend 30 minutes writing answers to these questions: What would you do differently if money were not a constraint? What experiences or activities do you most want your life to contain? What would financial security feel like, specifically — what would you stop worrying about? What would financial freedom allow you to do that you cannot do now? The answers reveal the specific life you are building toward, which provides motivation for the specific financial behaviors that build it. Abstract goals are weak motivators; vivid, specific pictures of your ideal financial life are strong ones.

Chapter 1 Exercise: Your Financial Values Inventory

Write down the three financial values that matter most to you — what you ultimately want money to provide in your life. These might be security, freedom, experiences, providing for family, charitable giving, or something else entirely. Then honestly assess: does your current financial behavior reflect these values, or does it reflect other priorities? The gap between stated values and actual financial behavior is where the most important work is.

Chapter Key Takeaways

- Financial behavior is driven more by psychology than by knowledge — addressing the psychology is essential
- Money scripts are unconscious beliefs from childhood that drive adult financial behavior; identifying yours is the first step to changing it
- Present bias, loss aversion, and mental accounting are cognitive biases that consistently produce poor financial decisions
- The gap between your stated financial values and your actual financial behavior is your most important diagnostic information
- Financial change requires understanding the emotional and psychological dimensions of money, not just better information

Notes — Chapter 1

CHAPTER 2

The Numbers That Actually Matter: Your Financial Baseline

You cannot improve what you haven't measured. Your financial baseline is the starting point for every financial decision.

Financial clarity begins with financial visibility. The discomfort of looking at your actual numbers — however far they are from where you want them to be — is the necessary starting point of every genuine financial improvement. There is no such thing as managing money you haven't counted.

The single most important financial act most people have never taken is sitting down and calculating their complete financial picture: what they earn, what they spend, what they own, and what they owe. This calculation — which takes about 90 minutes to complete thoroughly — produces the financial baseline from which all meaningful improvement begins.

Why Knowing Your Numbers Changes Everything

There is a documented phenomenon in financial behavior research: people who regularly review their financial numbers — net worth, savings rate, spending by category — make better financial decisions than people who avoid looking. The mechanism is not complicated: visibility creates accountability. When you know your numbers, financial choices feel more concrete and their long-term consequences more real.

Many people avoid knowing their financial numbers for the same reason some people avoid medical checkups — fear of what they might find. This avoidance is understandable but costly. Financial problems that are identified early are far easier to address than problems that have been allowed to compound through inattention. An accurate financial baseline, however uncomfortable, is always more useful than comfortable ignorance.

The Four Financial Numbers

Your financial life can be summarized in four numbers: monthly net income (what actually lands in your bank account), monthly expenses (what you actually spend), net worth (what you own minus what you owe), and your savings rate (the percentage of income you save and invest). These four numbers tell you more about your financial situation than any other metric.

Monthly Net Income

Net income is what you take home after taxes and any pre-tax deductions (401k contributions, health insurance premiums, FSA contributions). For people with variable income — freelancers, commission salespeople, business owners — use the average of the last 12 months of actual take-home income as your baseline, and plan using a conservative estimate rather than an optimistic one.

Monthly Expenses

Calculating actual monthly expenses requires looking at actual spending data — bank statements and credit card statements — rather than estimating from memory. Memory systematically underestimates spending on discretionary categories. Pull 3 months of statements and calculate your actual average monthly spending across all categories. This exercise almost always produces surprises — categories where actual spending significantly exceeds the mental estimate.

Net Worth

Net worth is the most comprehensive single measure of financial health: assets (checking, savings, investment accounts, retirement accounts, home equity, valuable property) minus liabilities (mortgage balance, car loan balances, student loan balances, credit card balances, any other debt). Many people avoid calculating their net worth because they fear it will be negative or lower than they expect. Negative net worth is common and is a starting point, not a verdict.

Savings Rate

The savings rate — what percentage of take-home income you save and invest each month — predicts wealth accumulation better than income level does. A household earning $50,000 with a 20% savings rate will accumulate significantly more wealth over a lifetime than a household earning $100,000 with a 5% savings rate. The target: work toward a 15–20% savings rate. Start wherever you are today, even if that is 1%.

The Net Worth Tracking Habit

Calculate your net worth once per month and record it. Many people use a simple spreadsheet with asset and liability columns; others use apps like Monarch Money, Copilot, or Empower Personal Dashboard. The monthly check-in takes 10 minutes and provides the most motivating feedback loop in personal finance: watching net worth trend upward month over month makes financial discipline feel worthwhile in a concrete, visible way.

Reading Your Pay Stub

Most people receive a paycheck or direct deposit notification without fully understanding where their gross income goes before it reaches their bank account. Understanding your pay stub is foundational financial literacy: it shows you exactly what you are paying in federal, state, and local taxes; what is being withheld for health insurance, retirement contributions, and other benefits; and what additional deductions are being taken. For many people, this calculation reveals that their effective take-home rate is significantly lower than their gross salary suggests — which is essential information for financial planning.

The most important number on your pay stub for planning purposes is your net income — what actually hits your bank account. Every financial plan, budget, and savings calculation should be based on net income, not gross income. Planning based on gross income and then adjusting for taxes is a common source of financial planning errors.

Understanding Your Tax Situation

Basic tax literacy produces meaningful financial benefits. Key concepts: your marginal tax rate (the rate you pay on your last dollar of income) is different from your effective tax rate (the average rate across all your income); pre-tax retirement contributions reduce your taxable income dollar for dollar; and the standard deduction vs. itemized deductions decision affects how much of your income is taxable. Even a basic understanding of these concepts can reduce your annual tax bill and improve your financial planning accuracy.

Reading Your Credit Report and Score

Your credit report is a record of your borrowing history maintained by the three major credit bureaus — Experian, TransUnion, and Equifax. Your credit score (most commonly the FICO score) is a numerical summary of this report, ranging from 300 to 850. Scores above 740 qualify for the best interest rates on mortgages, car loans, and other credit. Scores below 620 significantly limit borrowing options and increase the cost of credit.

Every American is entitled to a free credit report from each of the three bureaus every week at AnnualCreditReport.com — weekly access became permanent in 2023. Check yours annually for errors — which are more common than most people realize — and dispute any inaccurate negative items. The most important factors in your credit score: payment history (35%), amounts owed relative to available credit (30%), length of credit history (15%), credit mix (10%), and new credit inquiries (10%).

Financial Goal Setting That Actually Works

Most financial goal setting fails for the same reason most goal setting fails: goals are set in terms of outcomes (save $10,000, pay off debt, increase net worth) without the systems and intermediate steps that make those outcomes achievable. Outcome-based goals tell you where you want to go; system-based goals tell you what to do every day to get there.

SMART financial goals — Specific, Measurable, Achievable, Relevant, Time-bound — are an improvement over vague goals, but they are still outcome-focused. The most effective financial goals combine the SMART framework with a clear implementation plan: not just "save $5,000 this year" but "transfer $417/month automatically to my HYSA beginning this month, for 12 months." The plan converts the goal into a system.

Short, Medium, and Long-Term Financial Goals

A complete financial goal structure spans three time horizons. Short-term goals (1–2 years): emergency fund completion, high-interest debt elimination, specific savings targets like vacation or home downpayment. Medium-term goals (3–10 years): debt-free status, home purchase, specific net worth milestones, funding children's education. Long-term goals (10+ years): retirement readiness, financial independence, legacy goals. Each horizon requires different financial instruments and different levels of liquidity.

Net Worth Tracking: Your Single Most Important Financial Number

Net worth — total assets minus total liabilities — is the single number that most accurately represents your financial progress over time. Monthly income and expense tracking tells you about cash flow. Net worth tracking tells you whether your overall financial position is improving. A person who earns $80,000 per year but spends $82,000 and accumulates no assets has a negative net worth trend regardless of their income. A person who earns $50,000 per year, spends $42,000, and consistently saves the difference is building net worth even on a modest income.

Calculate and record your net worth monthly or quarterly. The trend is more important than the number: consistent upward movement, however gradual, indicates a financial system that is working. Negative or flat net worth trends despite adequate income indicate a spending or debt pattern that needs attention. Net worth tracking also makes invisible financial progress visible — the months when your investment accounts grow through market appreciation rather than new contributions still show up as net worth improvement, which provides motivational feedback that cash flow tracking alone cannot provide.

Understanding Cash Flow vs. Wealth

High income does not produce wealth; high income minus high expenses produces marginally positive or negative wealth depending on the difference. This distinction is obscured by cultural narratives that treat income as the primary measure of financial success. The research on wealth accumulation consistently shows that savings rate — the percentage of income saved and invested — predicts wealth accumulation far better than income level. That is why the savings-rate comparison earlier in this chapter comes out the way it does: the rate at which you save moves the result more than the size of the income it is drawn from.

The practical implication: focusing on income growth while neglecting savings rate is a common financial trap. Lifestyle inflation — the tendency for spending to expand to fill income — means that income increases often fail to improve financial position because they are accompanied by proportional spending increases. The most financially powerful habit is not earning more but maintaining savings rate as income grows, allowing lifestyle to improve while also increasing wealth accumulation rates.

The Financial Health Checkup

Just as physical health requires periodic checkups to catch problems early and track progress, financial health benefits from periodic review. A quarterly financial review covers: net worth change since the previous quarter, progress toward current financial goals, review of major spending categories against budget, and any upcoming financial decisions or life changes that require planning. A 30-minute quarterly review prevents the financial drift that turns a working system into a broken one over months of unattended accumulation.

The annual financial review is more comprehensive: reviewing insurance coverage for adequacy given any life changes, revisiting estate planning documents if circumstances have changed, reviewing investment allocations against target, assessing progress toward long-term goals, and setting financial targets for the coming year. People who conduct systematic financial reviews make better financial decisions, catch problems earlier, and report significantly less financial anxiety than those who manage finances reactively.

The One-Page Financial Dashboard

A one-page financial dashboard — a simple document that displays your most important financial metrics on a single page — is one of the most useful tools for maintaining financial clarity and motivation. The dashboard should include: current net worth and trend, current savings rate, emergency fund balance versus target, debt balances and monthly payoff progress, investment account balances and year-to-date growth, and progress toward your primary financial goal. Updating this dashboard monthly takes 15–20 minutes and provides the financial visibility that prevents the drift toward financial unawareness.

The motivational function of the dashboard is as important as the informational one. Seeing your net worth trend upward month after month, watching your debt balance decline, observing the compounding growth of your investment accounts — these visible indicators of progress provide the motivational reinforcement that sustains long-term financial behavior better than any abstract commitment to financial goals. What gets measured gets managed, and what gets measured also provides the feedback loops that keep financial behavior aligned with financial goals.

Chapter 2 Exercise: Calculate Your Financial Baseline

This week, calculate all four numbers: your monthly net income, your actual average monthly expenses (from 3 months of statements), your current net worth, and your current savings rate. Record them in a document or spreadsheet. If the numbers are discouraging, note that knowing your baseline is the essential first step — you cannot navigate from a location you haven't identified.

Chapter Key Takeaways

- The four financial numbers: monthly net income, monthly expenses, net worth, and savings rate
- Actual spending should be calculated from bank and credit card statements — memory underestimates consistently
- Net worth (assets minus liabilities) is the most comprehensive measure of financial health
- The savings rate predicts long-term wealth accumulation better than income level — target 15–20%
- Check your credit report annually for errors and monitor your credit score as a financial health indicator

Notes — Chapter 2

CHAPTER 3

Budgeting Without Misery: A System You Can Actually Maintain

A budget that you hate will fail. A system that fits your actual life — values, personality, and schedule — will work.

> ***"Do not save what is left after spending, but spend what is left after saving." — Warren Buffett (attributed)***

The fundamental shift from reactive budgeting (tracking where money went) to proactive spending planning (deciding where money goes) is one of the most important mindset changes in personal finance. It transforms the budget from an accounting tool into a values expression tool.

The word "budget" carries negative psychological associations for most people: restriction, sacrifice, complicated spreadsheets, tracking every penny, and guilt when you inevitably spend something "off-budget." These associations are largely a product of how budgeting has traditionally been presented — as a rigid, punishment-oriented system designed to minimize spending rather than to align spending with values.

Modern personal finance has moved toward a better framing: a spending plan — a proactive decision about where your money goes — rather than a budget — a reactive accounting of where it went. The goal is not maximum restriction; it is alignment between your spending and your values and priorities. Spending money on things you genuinely value is not a financial failure.

The True Cost of Spending

One of the most powerful reframings in personal finance is calculating the true cost of spending in hours worked rather than dollars. If your take-home hourly rate is $25/hour, a $500 purchase costs 20 hours of your life. If your savings rate is 10%, you need to work 10 hours to accumulate the savings equivalent of $250. These calculations don't necessarily change every purchase decision, but they reframe discretionary spending in terms of the resource that is ultimately most finite: your time and labor.

The "hours worked" framing is especially powerful for recurring expenses. A $150/month subscription that you use occasionally costs 6 hours of work per month — 72 hours (nearly two full work weeks) per year. Most people would not choose to work two weeks of overtime to maintain that subscription. But presented as $5/day, the same cost feels trivial. Translating recurring expenses into their annual cost and hours-worked equivalent often reveals spending patterns that monthly or weekly framing obscures.

The 50/30/20 Framework

The 50/30/20 rule, popularized by Senator Elizabeth Warren in her book All Your Worth, provides a simple allocation framework that works for most income levels: 50% of take-home income for needs (rent/mortgage, utilities, groceries, minimum debt payments, transportation, insurance), 30% for wants (restaurants, entertainment, travel, subscriptions, clothing beyond basics), and 20% for savings and debt paydown above minimums.

This framework is a starting point, not a rigid rule. High-cost-of-living cities may require 60–65% for needs. People aggressively paying down debt or building retirement savings may allocate 30–35% to that category. The value of the framework is in its simplicity: three categories that are easy to estimate and easy to evaluate against your actual spending.

The Anti-Budget System

Personal finance writer Paula Pant popularized the anti-budget system, which eliminates the complexity of category tracking entirely. The system has two steps: automate your savings and investments first, then spend freely on everything else. The math is simple: if you are saving and investing the right amount every month, your spending will automatically stay within acceptable bounds regardless of how it is categorized.

The anti-budget works because it addresses the most common budgeting failure mode: the gap between planning and execution. A comprehensive budget with 15 spending categories requires ongoing monitoring and produces guilt when categories are exceeded. An anti-budget requires setting up one or two automatic transfers and then forgetting about it — the discipline is baked into the system rather than requiring constant willpower.

Automate Everything

The most important financial automation: a transfer from checking to savings or investment account on the day your paycheck arrives, before you have an opportunity to spend the money. Set the amount to your target savings rate, then gradually increase it by 1% every 90 days. Most people don't notice small incremental reductions in available spending, but the compounding effect on savings over years is significant.

The Psychology of Successful Budgeting

Budgeting consistently fails not because the math is wrong but because it conflicts with human psychology in several important ways: it requires sustained vigilance against competing impulses; it surfaces uncomfortable information about spending; it can feel restrictive in ways that trigger reactive spending; and it requires consistent action where inaction is always the easier path. Effective spending plans are designed around these psychological realities rather than ignoring them.

The most psychologically effective financial systems share common design principles: they automate where possible, reducing the number of decisions required; they use positive framing (spend freely on what remains after saving) rather than negative framing (restrict yourself to category limits); they plan for occasional splurges rather than treating them as failures; and they are simple enough to maintain without significant ongoing time investment. Simplicity always beats sophistication in personal financial systems.

Sinking Funds: Planning for Known Future Expenses

One of the most practical budgeting tools is the sinking fund — a dedicated savings pool for a known future expense. Common sinking funds: car registration, annual insurance premiums, holiday gifts, annual vacations, home repairs, and property taxes if not escrowed. By saving a monthly amount toward these known future expenses, you eliminate the "surprise" large expense that disrupts budgets and forces debt use. A Christmas gift sinking fund of $100/month eliminates December credit card debt. A car repair sinking fund of $75/month eliminates the crisis of an unexpected mechanical failure.

Zero-Based Budgeting

Zero-based budgeting — the method used by popular apps like YNAB (You Need A Budget) — assigns every dollar of income to a specific category before spending begins, so that income minus all allocations equals zero. This system provides maximum control and visibility and is particularly valuable for people in active debt paydown mode or with tight margins between income and expenses. The tradeoff is that it requires more time and attention than simpler approaches.

Spending Categories Worth Tracking

Even for people who don't maintain a detailed budget, three categories warrant specific attention: food (eating out vs. groceries — restaurant spending is the most common source of budget leakage for working adults), subscriptions (recurring charges that accumulate invisibly — audit yours annually), and impulse purchases (unplanned purchases that individually seem small but collectively add up significantly). Awareness of actual spending in these three categories, even without a full budget, produces meaningful improvements in most people's financial outcomes.

Reducing Your Biggest Expenses

Frugality on small discretionary purchases — skipping lattes, canceling Netflix — produces psychologically satisfying but financially minimal impact. The most significant spending reductions come from the big three: housing (typically 25–35% of income for most households), transportation (typically 15–20%), and food (typically 10–15%). A 10% reduction in any of these categories produces 4–10x the savings of eliminating all small discretionary purchases.

Housing is the highest-leverage expense to optimize. For renters, the most impactful decisions are location choice (rent varies dramatically across neighborhoods and cities) and space allocation (fewer square feet means lower rent, utilities, and furnishing costs). For homeowners, refinancing when rates drop significantly, making additional principal payments, and resisting the temptation to "upsize" to a home that stretches affordability all have major long-term financial impacts.

The Transportation Optimization

Transportation is typically the second-largest household expense and one of the most susceptible to cost reduction. The single most impactful transportation decision: vehicle choice. Buying a reliable used vehicle outright (or with a minimal loan at a low rate) rather than financing a new or newer vehicle produces savings of $5,000–$10,000 or more over a 5-year period compared to buying new. Adding commute optimization (remote work, transit, cycling for short commutes) can produce thousands more in additional savings annually.

The Psychology of Spending Decisions

Spending decisions are rarely purely rational calculations of value. They are shaped by cognitive biases, emotional states, social influences, and the mental accounting shortcuts that the brain uses to manage the cognitive overhead of constant financial decision-making. Understanding these influences is not about eliminating emotion from spending — emotion is an appropriate input to decisions about how to spend your limited resources. It is about preventing the specific cognitive patterns that consistently produce spending regret.

The most financially costly cognitive pattern is present bias: the tendency to overweight immediate gratification relative to future benefit. Present bias explains why people make financial decisions that their future selves will regret, why diets start Monday and why retirement savings get deferred until "when I have more money." Structural interventions — automating savings before the money becomes available to spend, using friction to create delay before discretionary purchases, separating money for specific purposes into separate accounts — address present bias at the system level rather than requiring constant vigilance.

Building a Personalized Spending Plan

A spending plan that works is one that reflects your actual values and priorities, not the values you believe you should have. This distinction matters because a budget built around aspirational values creates constant friction — you are planning to spend in ways that conflict with what you actually want — while a budget built around your genuine priorities creates alignment between your financial behavior and your life. The person who values experiences over possessions builds a spending plan that allocates generously to travel and social activities while minimizing spending on clothes and furniture. The person who values home environment allocates accordingly.

The practical approach: before building your spending plan, identify your three to five highest spending priorities — the categories where your spending most consistently reflects genuine satisfaction rather than impulse or habit. Allocate adequately to these first, then reduce spending in the categories that provide less satisfaction per dollar. This values-based approach to spending produces a budget you can actually sustain, because you are aligning your financial behavior with what matters to you rather than with what you think should matter to you.

Who the Anti-Budget Works For

For people who find traditional detailed budgeting demotivating, the anti-budget is a simpler alternative that produces similar outcomes with less maintenance. The anti-budget has two steps: first, automate all savings and investment contributions at the beginning of each month. Second, spend the remainder as you choose without tracking individual categories. The structure ensures the most important financial behaviors — savings and investment — happen automatically, while providing freedom in discretionary spending that many people find more sustainable than line-item tracking.

The anti-budget works best for people whose spending problem is not impulse purchasing but under-saving. It does not work well for people with significant debt who need to maximize debt payoff or for people whose spending patterns include categories they genuinely want to reduce. For those situations, some version of tracking and category awareness is necessary. But for the substantial portion of people who are adequate spenders but inadequate savers, the anti-budget eliminates the most frustrating aspect of budgeting while preserving its most important effect.

Setting Up a Sinking Fund

Car insurance renewals, holiday gifts, annual subscriptions, vacations, and irregular home expenses are predictable in that they will occur, even if the precise timing is uncertain. Most people handle these expenses reactively — scrambling to cover them when they arrive, often by deferring other financial priorities or adding to credit card balances. Sinking funds convert irregular large expenses into manageable regular savings contributions.

The mechanics are simple: identify your major annual irregular expenses, add them up, and divide by 12. This monthly amount is your sinking fund contribution, automatically transferred to a dedicated savings account (or a designated bucket within a single high-yield savings account). When the irregular expense arrives, you have the money waiting. The relief of not scrambling to cover predictable expenses is significant, and the elimination of the credit card debt that often covers these expenses produces both financial and psychological improvement

Chapter 3 Exercise: Design Your Spending Plan

Based on your income and expense baseline from Chapter 2, design a spending plan using whichever framework resonates most. Identify your savings allocation first and automate it. Then assess whether your remaining spending is aligned with your stated financial values from Chapter 1. Identify one category where spending could be reduced without meaningfully reducing your quality of life, and one category where spending could be increased to better reflect your actual priorities.

Chapter Key Takeaways

- A spending plan — a proactive allocation of income — produces better results than a reactive budget
- The 50/30/20 framework (needs/wants/savings) provides a simple starting allocation to assess against
- The anti-budget system: automate savings first, then spend freely — discipline is built into the system
- Zero-based budgeting provides maximum control and is particularly useful during active debt paydown
- Food, subscriptions, and impulse purchases are the three categories most worth tracking even without a full budget

Notes — Chapter 3

CHAPTER 4

Debt: Understanding It, Prioritizing It, Eliminating It

Not all debt is equal. Understanding the difference between debt that costs you and debt that can serve you is one of the most important financial skills.

> ***"The rich ruleth over the poor, and the borrower is servant to the lender." — Proverbs 22:7***

Consumer debt is not simply an inconvenience — it is a structural constraint that redirects your future income to pay for your past consumption. Every month that high-interest debt is carried, a portion of your earning potential is pre-committed to a creditor rather than available for your own financial goals. Understanding this constraint in concrete terms is often the motivation that drives aggressive paydown.

Debt is the single most powerful obstacle to financial progress for most Americans. The combination of high interest rates on consumer debt, the psychological burden of owing money, and the compounding effect of interest charges that grow the balance even when payments are made consistently — this combination keeps millions of people in financial stagnation for years or decades.

The Psychological Weight of Debt Freedom

People who have paid off significant consumer debt almost universally describe the experience as more psychologically transformative than they anticipated. The sense of agency, security, and possibility that accompanies debt freedom is qualitatively different from the incremental relief of each monthly payment — it represents a fundamental shift in the relationship between income and options.

This psychological payoff is worth pursuing even when a purely rational analysis might suggest that low-rate debt is less urgent than high-yield investments. For people who find their debt psychologically burdensome — who think about it frequently, whose financial anxiety is closely tied to their debt level — accelerating payoff beyond what the math strictly requires can produce well-being benefits that justify the financial cost.

Good Debt vs. Bad Debt

The distinction between good debt and bad debt is not absolute, but it is useful: good debt finances assets that appreciate in value or generate income (a carefully underwritten mortgage on a home in a reasonable market, student loans that produce a meaningful return in earned income), and typically carries lower interest rates. Bad debt finances consumption — spending on things that depreciate or are consumed immediately — and typically carries high interest rates.

Credit card debt at 18–29% APR is the clearest example of bad debt. Car loans for vehicles that exceed what your financial situation reasonably supports are another. Personal loans used to fund lifestyle spending are another. The reason bad debt is financially devastating is compound interest working in reverse: at 20% APR a balance left untouched doubles in about three and a half years, and a balance serviced only with minimum payments — which are mostly interest — takes the better part of two decades to clear.

The Avalanche Method

The avalanche method prioritizes debts by interest rate, paying the minimum on all debts while directing every additional dollar toward the highest-rate debt. Once the highest-rate debt is paid off, the full payment amount (minimum plus extra) is redirected to the next-highest-rate debt, creating an accelerating payoff cascade. The avalanche method is mathematically optimal — it minimizes total interest paid over the payoff period.

The Snowball Method

The snowball method, popularized by Dave Ramsey, prioritizes debts by balance size — smallest first regardless of interest rate. The psychological logic: eliminating individual debts creates a sense of momentum and accomplishment that motivates continued effort. Research by Blake McShane and David Gal at Northwestern, and by Remi Trudel at Boston University, found that the snowball method actually produces better real-world results for many people than the mathematically superior avalanche method — because behavior drives outcomes more than math does.

The Hybrid Approach

Combine the best of both methods: if your lowest-balance debt and your highest-interest debt are different debts, pay off the lowest-balance debt first to generate momentum, then switch to the avalanche method for all remaining debts. This hybrid captures the motivational benefits of the snowball for the first win while minimizing total interest paid for all subsequent payoffs.

The Hidden Costs of Debt

The financial cost of debt — the interest payments — is visible and calculable. The psychological cost is less visible but equally significant. Research on the psychology of debt consistently finds that carrying high-interest consumer debt is associated with elevated cortisol levels, reduced sleep quality, impaired cognitive function, relationship conflict, and reduced self-reported well-being. These psychological costs compound the financial costs and create a negative feedback loop: stress impairs the decision-making and impulse control that would reduce spending and accelerate debt payoff.

Understanding the full cost of debt — financial plus psychological — often provides the motivational urgency that purely financial calculations don't. The person who recognizes that their credit card debt is costing them not just $2,400/year in interest but also chronic background stress, sleep disruption, and relationship tension is more likely to make the sacrifices required for aggressive paydown than the person who sees only the interest charge.

Avoiding Debt Relapse

The most common reason people who pay off consumer debt re-accumulate it is that they did not address the underlying spending pattern that created the debt in the first place. Debt payoff without behavioral change produces temporary results. Sustainable debt freedom requires identifying which spending categories drove the original debt accumulation, understanding the emotional or habitual drivers of that spending, and designing a system that addresses those drivers structurally.

Negotiating Lower Interest Rates

Most people don't know that credit card interest rates are negotiable. Cardholders with a good payment history who call their card issuer and ask for a lower rate often get one, and the request costs nothing. The call takes about 10 minutes. Prepare by knowing your current rate, your payment history, and any competing offers you've received. A 5-percentage-point reduction on a $10,000 balance saves $500 per year in interest.

Student Loans: A Special Case

Student loan debt requires case-by-case analysis because the variables — interest rate, loan type (federal vs. private), income trajectory, and career field — differ significantly between borrowers. Key decision points: whether income-driven repayment plans or Public Service Loan Forgiveness (PSLF) apply to your situation; whether refinancing federal loans to private loans makes sense for your income security and forgiveness eligibility; and how aggressively to pay down student loans vs. investing, which depends on the interest rate relative to expected investment returns.

The Credit Score Optimization Plan

Your credit score affects the interest rates you pay on mortgages, car loans, and other credit — potentially saving or costing you tens of thousands of dollars over a lifetime. The good news: credit score improvement follows predictable principles that most people can implement without specialized help.

- Pay on time, every time: Payment history is 35% of your score. Set up autopay for at least the minimum payment on every account to eliminate late payments.
- Keep utilization below 30%: Credit utilization (balance as % of limit) is 30% of your score. If your utilization is above 30%, paying down balances or requesting credit limit increases (without using the additional credit) will improve your score.
- Don't close old accounts: Length of credit history affects your score. Closing old accounts reduces your average account age and your available credit, potentially harming your score.
- Limit new credit applications: Each hard credit inquiry reduces your score by a few points. Apply for new credit only when necessary.

The Emotional Cost of Debt

Debt costs more than interest: it also costs flexibility and forecloses future options. The emotional cost is equally real and often equally significant, but less discussed. Carrying debt, particularly high-interest consumer debt, creates a chronic low-level financial anxiety that affects well-being, relationship quality, and cognitive performance. The relief that people describe when they pay off significant debt is not just financial — it is a genuine reduction in psychological burden.

This emotional cost is worth accounting for in debt payoff decisions. The mathematically optimal debt payoff strategy (highest interest rate first) may not be the psychologically optimal one. For some people, the motivation provided by a quick early win — paying off a small balance first to feel the psychological relief of a zero balance — produces better long-term follow-through than the mathematically superior avalanche method. Your debt payoff strategy should account for your psychology as well as your interest rates. The strategy you will actually follow for two years beats the strategy that is theoretically optimal but requires willpower you cannot sustain.

What Else Is Negotiable: Medical and Student Debt

Most people treat the interest rates and terms on existing debt as fixed facts rather than negotiable variables. They are often negotiable, and the effort required to attempt negotiation is small relative to the potential savings. Credit card companies regularly reduce interest rates for customers who call and request reductions, particularly for accounts in good standing. Medical debt is almost always negotiable and providers have established processes for reducing balances for patients who request financial hardship consideration. Student loan servicers have income-based repayment options and forgiveness programs that many borrowers never access because they do not know to ask.

A ten-minute phone call that reduces your credit card interest rate from 22% to 16% saves roughly $300 on a $5,000 balance over a two-year payoff period, and proportionally more on a larger one. Researching the hardship programs, rate reduction processes, and income-based options available on your specific debts is one of the highest-return financial activities available. The information is public; the barrier is knowing it exists and asking for it.

Credit Reports and Credit Monitoring

Your credit report — the detailed record of your credit history maintained by the three major credit bureaus — is the foundation of your credit score. You are entitled to a free credit report from each bureau every week through AnnualCreditReport.com. Reviewing your reports annually for errors, fraudulent accounts, and inaccurate negative items is an important financial maintenance activity. Credit report errors are common and can significantly impact your score; disputing them is a straightforward process that produces score improvements when errors are corrected.

Credit monitoring services — which alert you to changes in your credit report in near-real-time — are valuable for detecting identity theft quickly. Several free options are available through major credit card companies and standalone services.

The cost-benefit calculus: monitoring is worth the few minutes required to set it up for anyone who has experienced identity theft or who has concerns about their data security. For most people with stable credit and no history of identity theft, the free annual credit report review is sufficient.

Debt and Mental Health: The Psychological Weight of What You Owe

Research on the relationship between debt and mental health is striking: people with high debt relative to assets report significantly higher rates of depression and anxiety, impaired cognitive function related to financial worry, and lower life satisfaction than those with comparable incomes but lower debt. This relationship is causal in both directions — financial stress produces mental health consequences, and mental health challenges can impair the financial decision-making that would address the underlying debt.

This mental health dimension of debt is worth factoring into debt payoff strategy. The psychological relief of eliminating even one debt entirely — the experience of having zero balance on a credit card, the freedom from a monthly payment — produces well-being improvements that the interest savings calculation alone does not capture. For people experiencing significant financial anxiety, the debt payoff strategy that provides the fastest psychological relief may be worth more than the one that provides the fastest mathematical debt elimination, because the psychological relief improves the decision-making capacity that supports continued progress.

Chapter 4 Exercise: Your Debt Payoff Plan

List all your debts with current balance, interest rate, and minimum monthly payment. Calculate the total interest you will pay if you make only minimum payments. Then design a payoff plan using either the avalanche or snowball method. Calculate how much faster you could pay off all debt by adding $200/month to your paydown — this calculation is often motivating enough to prompt finding that extra $200.

Chapter Key Takeaways

- Consumer debt at high interest rates is one of the most powerful destroyers of financial progress
- The avalanche method (highest rate first) minimizes total interest paid; the snowball method (smallest balance first) maximizes motivational momentum
- Credit card interest rates are frequently negotiable — a 10-minute phone call can produce meaningful savings
- Student loan strategy depends on interest rate, loan type, and career trajectory — federal loans carry options that private loans don't
- Every dollar above the minimum payment on high-interest debt produces a guaranteed tax-free return equal to the debt's interest rate

Notes — Chapter 4

CHAPTER 5

The Emergency Fund: Your Financial Foundation

An emergency fund is not a savings account. It is insurance against financial catastrophe that protects every other financial goal.

An emergency fund is the foundation of financial freedom.

Financial security is built in layers, and the emergency fund is the ground floor. Without it, you are one unexpected expense away from adding to your debt load regardless of how well you've managed everything else. With it, you have a buffer that allows every other financial plan to operate as designed even when life doesn't cooperate.

Every personal finance framework, regardless of its other priorities or philosophies, includes the emergency fund as a foundational element — and with good reason. Without an emergency fund, any unexpected expense — a car repair, a medical bill, a job loss — immediately becomes a debt event.

The absence of cash reserves forces people to borrow money at high interest rates to handle normal life expenses, creating a debt spiral that undermines every other financial goal.

The Most Common Emergency Fund Mistakes

Three mistakes account for most emergency fund failures. First, building the fund too slowly — contributing $25/month to an account that needs $10,000 means a 33-year timeline. Set a completion target and work backward to a monthly contribution that achieves it within 12–18 months. Second, using the wrong account — a checking account or low-yield savings account costs hundreds of dollars per year in foregone interest at current high-yield savings rates. Third, using the fund for non-emergencies — vacation financing, gifts, and planned annual expenses are not emergencies and should have their own dedicated sinking funds.

How Much Is Enough

The standard recommendation is three to six months of essential living expenses — the amount you would need to cover rent/mortgage, utilities, groceries, insurance, and minimum debt payments for three to six months without any income. Three months is the minimum; six months is appropriate for people with variable income, less stable employment, or health conditions that create medical expense risk. Single-income households generally benefit from a larger fund than dual-income households.

A more accessible target for people starting from zero: a $1,000 starter emergency fund that you build before aggressively paying down debt. This amount handles the most common emergencies (car repairs, small medical bills, minor home repairs) without requiring debt. Once high-interest debt is eliminated, build to the full 3–6 month target.

Where to Keep It

The emergency fund belongs in a high-yield savings account at an online bank, kept separate from your primary checking account. The separation creates just enough friction to stop the fund being spent casually, while the money stays accessible within one to two business days. High-yield accounts pay substantially more interest than traditional bank savings accounts — enough that a fully funded emergency fund earns hundreds of dollars a year that a checking account would not — and they carry the same FDIC insurance protection up to $250,000. Rates move with prevailing interest rates, so compare current offers rather than assuming the one you opened years ago is still competitive.

The Emergency Fund Automation

Build your emergency fund through automatic monthly transfers — even small ones. A $100/month automatic transfer builds a $1,200 starter fund in one year without requiring any ongoing decision-making. Once the fund reaches your target, redirect that automatic transfer to your investment accounts. The key is that the transfer happens automatically, before you have the opportunity to spend the money.

The Financial Security Mindset

Having an adequate emergency fund produces a measurable psychological effect that goes beyond the practical protection it provides: it changes your relationship with risk, with your employer, and with financial decisions generally. People with adequate financial reserves make better financial decisions — they are less vulnerable to predatory financial products, more willing to walk away from bad deals, and better able to take calculated risks that can improve their financial situation.

The security mindset that a healthy emergency fund produces is also protective against financial manipulation. High-pressure sales tactics, "act now or lose forever" offers, and exploitative financial products all gain their power from financial urgency — the feeling that you cannot afford to say no. An adequate emergency fund removes that urgency and restores your negotiating position in every financial transaction.

Tiered Emergency Savings

Some financial planners recommend a tiered emergency savings structure that differentiates between truly liquid reserves and slightly less liquid but higher-yield reserves. Tier 1: 1 month of expenses in a standard savings account for immediate access. Tier 2: 2–5 additional months in a high-yield savings account or short-term CDs for slightly higher returns while maintaining accessibility. This tiered approach captures higher interest rates on the bulk of the fund while maintaining genuine liquidity for immediate emergencies.

What Counts as an Emergency

Defining in advance what constitutes an appropriate use of the emergency fund prevents the gradual erosion that drains many emergency funds. True emergencies: job loss or significant income reduction, medical emergencies not covered by insurance, essential vehicle or home repairs that cannot be safely deferred, unexpected essential travel (family medical emergency). Not emergencies: planned expenses you forgot to budget for, sale prices on desired items, vacations, gifts, or any expense that could be anticipated and saved for in advance.

Rebuilding After a Withdrawal

After using your emergency fund for a genuine emergency, rebuilding it should become your highest financial priority — above additional debt paydown and above non-essential investment contributions. An empty emergency fund while carrying consumer debt and continuing to invest is an inconsistent position: you are earning lower investment returns than you are paying in interest, and you are fully exposed to the next unexpected expense becoming a new debt event.

Building Financial Resilience Beyond the Emergency Fund

Financial resilience — the capacity to absorb financial shocks without derailing your long-term financial progress — is the goal that the emergency fund partially addresses but doesn't fully achieve alone. Complete financial resilience requires: adequate insurance coverage (so that medical or property catastrophes don't produce financial ruin), multiple income streams (so that the loss of any single income source doesn't create a crisis), and adequate liquid reserves (so that short-term income disruptions can be bridged without debt).

The emergency fund is the most liquid element of financial resilience. It handles the most common shocks. The other elements — insurance, income diversification — handle the less common but more severe shocks that an emergency fund alone cannot address. Building complete financial resilience requires attention to all three layers.

The Financial Safety Net Review

Once per year, review your complete financial safety net: the size of your emergency fund relative to your current expenses (expenses change), your insurance coverage relative to your current assets and obligations (these change too), and your income concentration (how dependent are you on a single employer or client?). This annual review ensures your safety net keeps pace with your life's evolution.

Psychological Benefits of Financial Resilience

Research on financial resilience consistently shows that the buffer provided by liquid savings changes people's relationship with risk throughout their financial life. With no emergency fund, every financial decision is made against a backdrop of potential catastrophe — a perception that distorts risk assessment and leads to both excessive conservatism (avoiding investments that would build long-term wealth) and excessive impulsiveness (making poor financial decisions to escape anxiety). With an adequate emergency fund, financial decisions can be evaluated on their actual merits rather than through the distorting lens of scarcity anxiety.

The Savings Rate Imperative

The single financial habit with the greatest long-term impact is a consistent savings rate — saving and investing a defined percentage of every paycheck regardless of what else is happening financially. This habit, implemented through automation, addresses the primary obstacle to consistent saving: the tendency to save whatever is left after spending rather than spend whatever is left after saving. When saving is automatic and happens before discretionary spending decisions, it is not subject to the moment-to-moment negotiations that erode discretionary savings intentions.

Even a modest savings rate, applied consistently over decades, produces outcomes that seem counterintuitive. Saving 10% of income, invested in diversified index funds, for 30 years produces a balance that typically exceeds the total income earned over that period — because the compounding of returns on invested capital eventually overwhelms the contributions. This is not a get-rich-quick formula; it is the predictable result of the mathematics of compound growth applied over long time horizons. The people who build genuine wealth through ordinary means almost universally share this one habit: consistent, automated saving at a meaningful rate, started as early as possible.

Why Your Emergency Fund Stays Out of the Market

Do not invest your emergency fund in the stock market or other volatile assets. The emergency fund's purpose is liquidity and stability — the ability to access the full amount immediately when needed, regardless of market conditions. A market downturn that reduces your emergency fund value by 30% at the moment you need it most (often during a job loss, when markets may also be declining) defeats its purpose entirely. High-yield savings accounts provide a meaningful interest advantage with the stability and liquidity that emergency funds require.

Chapter 5 Exercise: Emergency Fund Action Plan

Calculate your monthly essential expenses. Multiply by 3 for your minimum target and by 6 for your full target. If you don't yet have a high-yield savings account, open one this week — the process takes 10 minutes online. Set up a recurring automatic transfer in whatever amount you can commit to. If you already have an adequate emergency fund, redirect any funds above 6 months of expenses to investment accounts.

Chapter Key Takeaways

- An emergency fund prevents any unexpected expense from becoming a debt event
- Target: $1,000 starter fund first, then 3–6 months of essential expenses when high-interest debt is cleared
- Keep the emergency fund in a high-yield savings account — accessible but separate from day-to-day spending
- Define "emergency" in advance to protect the fund from gradual erosion through non-emergency use
- After any withdrawal, rebuilding the emergency fund becomes the highest financial priority

Notes — Chapter 5

CHAPTER 6

Investing Basics: Making Your Money Work While You Sleep

Investing is not gambling. It is the disciplined, patient application of compound growth to produce long-term wealth.

> ***"The stock market is a device for transferring money from the impatient to the patient." — Warren Buffett (attributed)***

Long-term investing success requires primarily two things: starting, and continuing. The sophistication of your investment strategy matters far less than the consistency of your contributions and your discipline during market downturns. This chapter gives you the simplest evidence-based approach to investing — one that has consistently outperformed more sophisticated alternatives.

The word "investing" intimidates many people into inaction — conjuring images of stock traders, complex financial instruments, and incomprehensible market movements. This framing serves Wall Street's interests (complicated investing requires paid advisors) but not individual investors'. The evidence-based approach to individual investing is simple enough to explain in one chapter and implement in an afternoon.

The Investment Account Types Explained

The three primary investment account types available to individual investors differ primarily in their tax treatment. Taxable brokerage accounts have no contribution limits and no restrictions on withdrawals, but investment gains are subject to capital gains taxes. Tax-deferred accounts (traditional IRAs, 401(k)s) reduce taxable income in the contribution year but require paying income tax on withdrawals. Tax-exempt accounts (Roth IRAs, Roth 401(k)s) don't reduce current taxable income but allow tax-free withdrawal of both contributions and growth.

The optimal combination depends on your current tax rate, expected retirement tax rate, timeline, and whether you need flexibility to access funds before retirement. The general guidance: maximize tax-advantaged accounts before using taxable accounts, and choose between traditional and Roth based on your assessment of whether you are in a higher or lower tax bracket now than you expect to be in retirement.

Compound Growth: The Most Important Concept in Personal Finance

Compound growth — earning returns on your returns — is the mechanism by which small, consistent investments produce large long-term wealth. The Rule of 72 provides a quick estimate of compound growth: divide 72 by the expected annual return to find how many years it takes for an investment to double. At a 7% average annual return (approximately the long-term historical inflation-adjusted return of the US stock market), investments double approximately every 10.3 years.

The practical implication of compound growth is that starting early is far more valuable than starting with more money. A 25-year-old who invests $200/month for 40 years at 7% will have approximately $528,000 at retirement. A 35-year-old who invests $400/month for 30 years at 7% — twice as much per month for 10 fewer years — will have approximately $486,000. Starting early wins even when the monthly contribution is half as large.

Index Funds: The Evidence-Based Choice

Decades of financial research have converged on a clear finding: the majority of actively managed investment funds — funds run by professional stock pickers who select individual securities — underperform simple passive index funds over time. This finding, which has been replicated across markets, time periods, and fund categories, reflects the efficiency of financial markets: it is very difficult for anyone, including professional investors, to consistently identify mispricings before the market corrects them.

Index funds solve this problem by not trying to beat the market. They simply hold every security in a given index (such as the S&P 500, which represents the 500 largest US companies) in proportion to their market weight. Because index funds don't require expensive active management, their costs (expense ratios) are a fraction of actively managed fund costs — typically 0.03–0.10% annually vs. 0.5–1.5% for actively managed funds. These cost differences compound dramatically over long investment horizons.

The Three-Fund Portfolio

The simplest evidence-based investment portfolio consists of three index funds: a US total market index fund, an international total market index fund, and a US total bond market index fund. The allocation between stocks and bonds depends on your time horizon and risk tolerance — more stocks for longer horizons and higher risk tolerance, more bonds as you approach the need for the money. Vanguard, Fidelity, and Schwab all offer low-cost versions of these three funds.

Common Investing Mistakes to Avoid

The evidence on investing outcomes consistently shows that investor behavior — specifically, the tendency to buy when markets are high and sell when they're low — is the primary determinant of poor investment returns. The most important investing mistakes are behavioral, not analytical:

- Checking portfolio values too frequently: Frequent monitoring amplifies the emotional response to normal volatility and increases the probability of reactive, poorly-timed decisions. Monthly or quarterly review is sufficient for most long-term investors.
- Chasing past performance: Investment funds that performed best last year are not more likely to outperform this year. Research consistently shows that past fund performance is a poor predictor of future performance.
- Over-concentration in employer stock: Holding a significant portion of your retirement portfolio in your employer's stock creates a dangerous correlation between your human capital (your job) and your financial capital. If the company struggles, both your income and your retirement savings decline simultaneously.
- Market timing: Attempting to move money in and out of investments based on market conditions — even with research and analysis — reliably underperforms a simple buy-and-hold approach.

Dollar-Cost Averaging

Dollar-cost averaging — investing a fixed amount at regular intervals regardless of market conditions — is the investment strategy most appropriate for the majority of individual investors. It removes the pressure of "timing the market" (trying to invest at market lows and sell at highs, which even professional investors reliably fail to do consistently) by making market timing irrelevant. When markets are down, your fixed investment buys more shares. When markets are up, it buys fewer. Over time, your average purchase price reflects the long-term market trend rather than the specific conditions on any individual purchase date.

Asset Allocation and Rebalancing

Asset allocation — how you divide your investment portfolio among different asset classes (stocks, bonds, cash, real estate) — is the most important investment decision you make. Research by Gary Brinson and colleagues found that asset allocation explains approximately 90% of portfolio return variability over time — more than security selection, market timing, or any other investment decision.

The appropriate stock/bond allocation depends primarily on your time horizon. A common guideline: subtract your age from 110 to get your target stock allocation percentage (a 30-year-old would target approximately 80% stocks, 20% bonds). More aggressive versions subtract from 120 or 130; more conservative versions subtract from 100. Within your stock allocation, broad diversification across geographies (US and international) and company sizes (large, mid, and small cap) is achieved automatically with total market index funds.

Rebalancing

Over time, different asset classes grow at different rates, shifting your portfolio away from your target allocation. Rebalancing — selling overweight assets and buying underweight ones to return to target allocation — maintains your intended risk level. Annual rebalancing is sufficient for most investors. A practical approach: rebalance when any asset class drifts more than 5 percentage points from its target, or review annually and rebalance if needed. Tax-advantaged accounts are the best place to rebalance since transactions don't trigger taxable events.

The Investor Psychology Problem

The average investor in US stock funds has historically underperformed the funds themselves by 1–2% annually, because investors buy after markets rise and sell after markets fall — doing exactly the opposite of what produces good returns. This performance gap is not caused by bad investment selection; it is caused by the emotional responses to market volatility that lead investors to abandon their strategies at precisely the worst times. Understanding this behavioral problem is as important as understanding any specific investment strategy.

The research on investor behavior consistently shows that the investors who achieve the best long-term outcomes are not those with the most sophisticated strategies — they are those who do the least. People who invest regularly, diversify broadly, hold for decades, and ignore short-term market movements outperform active investors and market-timers at every level of sophistication. The behavioral discipline to stay invested through market downturns — to not check your portfolio's daily value, to not sell when the news is frightening — is worth more than any specific investment selection skill.

Building an Investment Policy Statement

An investment policy statement is a written document that defines your investment approach, asset allocation, rebalancing rules, and the principles you have committed to follow. Its primary value is not as a planning document — it is as an anchor document for market volatility. When markets fall 20% and every financial news outlet is predicting further declines, a written commitment to your investment principles prevents the panic-driven decisions that produce the investor behavior gap described above.

A personal investment policy statement for a long-term investor covers: your investment goals and time horizons, your target asset allocation (percentage in stocks, bonds, and other asset classes), your rebalancing rules (when you will rebalance and how), your rules for adding new investments, and your rules for not selling (the conditions under which you have committed in advance not to sell). The last element is the most important. A policy statement that specifies "I will not sell equity investments in response to market declines of less than 40% within a 12-month period" gives you a decision rule to consult rather than an emotional state to manage when markets are falling.

What the Performance Data Shows

The evidence that index funds outperform actively managed funds over long time periods is extensive and consistent. Studies by Vanguard, S&P Dow Jones, and multiple academic researchers consistently find that 80–90% of actively managed mutual funds underperform their benchmark index over 10-year periods, and over 90% underperform over 20-year periods. The underperformance is primarily attributable to management fees, transaction costs, and the difficulty of consistently identifying mispriced securities in a highly competitive market.

The implication for individual investors is clear: a simple portfolio of low-cost index funds will, over the long term, outperform the portfolios of most professional money managers. This is not because index investors are more skilled — it is because they capture market returns at minimal cost while active managers incur costs that reduce returns below market levels. The simplest effective investment strategy available to individual investors — regular contributions to a total market index fund — is also one of the most powerful.

Tax-Efficient Investing: Keeping More of What You Earn

Investment returns and investment taxes are both real variables in long-term wealth building. A portfolio that earns 7% annually but generates significant taxable distributions produces lower after-tax returns than a portfolio that earns 6.5% in a tax-efficient structure. The difference compounds dramatically over time. Tax efficiency in investing is achieved through several strategies: using tax-advantaged accounts (401(k), IRA, HSA) for the most tax-inefficient assets (bonds, REITs, actively managed funds), holding tax-efficient investments (broad market index funds, growth stocks held long-term) in taxable accounts, and harvesting tax losses in taxable accounts to offset gains.

The asset location strategy — holding specific types of investments in the accounts where their tax treatment is most advantageous — is one of the most consistently underutilized free sources of return improvement available to individual investors. Bonds, which generate interest taxed at ordinary income rates, belong in tax-deferred retirement accounts. US total market index funds, which are highly tax-efficient due to low turnover and qualified dividends, can be held efficiently in taxable accounts. REITs, which generate non-qualified dividends taxed at ordinary income rates, belong in tax-advantaged accounts. Implementing this asset location strategy adds an estimated 0.5–1.5% annually in after-tax returns over a portfolio with random asset location.

Chapter 6 Exercise: Set Up Your First Investment Account

If you don't already invest, open a brokerage account this week (Fidelity, Vanguard, and Schwab are all excellent low-cost options). Purchase a total US market index fund with whatever amount you are comfortable starting with. Set up an automatic monthly investment in the same fund. If you already invest, review your expense ratios — if any funds have expense ratios above 0.5%, research lower-cost alternatives.

Chapter Key Takeaways

- Compound growth makes early investing dramatically more valuable than later investing with larger amounts
- Index funds consistently outperform the majority of actively managed funds over time, at a fraction of the cost
- The three-fund portfolio (US stocks, international stocks, bonds) provides diversification with minimal complexity
- Dollar-cost averaging — investing fixed amounts at regular intervals — removes market timing pressure
- Staying invested through market downturns is the most important investment discipline — behavior drives returns more than selection

Notes — Chapter 6

CHAPTER 7

Retirement Accounts: The Best Deal in Personal Finance

Tax-advantaged retirement accounts are the single most powerful legal tool available to individual wealth builders. Using them is not optional for anyone serious about financial security.

"Compound interest is the eighth wonder of the world." — Albert Einstein (attributed)

Tax-advantaged retirement accounts are the vehicle through which compound growth produces its most dramatic effects. Understanding them fully — and using them to their maximum — is one of the clearest ways to distinguish financially sophisticated behavior from financially naive behavior, regardless of income level.

Tax-advantaged retirement accounts — 401(k)s, IRAs, Roth IRAs, and their variants — represent a legal subsidy of your wealth building by the government. The tax benefits they provide, compounded over a 30–40 year investment horizon, add up to hundreds of thousands of dollars in additional wealth compared to investing the same amounts in a taxable brokerage account. Not taking advantage of these accounts is one of the most consequential financial mistakes an individual can make.

The Time Value of Retirement Savings

The mathematical case for starting retirement savings as early as possible is compelling, but its full force is often not appreciated because the time periods involved are so long that they don't feel real. A concrete illustration: $1,000 invested at age 25 at a 7% average annual return becomes approximately $14,974 by age 65 — without any additional contributions. The same $1,000 invested at age 45 becomes $3,870. The 20-year difference produces a nearly 4-fold difference in outcomes.

Applied to realistic contribution levels: a 25-year-old who contributes $5,000/year to a Roth IRA for 40 years (total contributions: $200,000) will have approximately $998,000 at 65 at a 7% average return. A 35-year-old who contributes $10,000/year for 30 years (total contributions: $300,000) — contributing 50% more — will have approximately $945,000. Starting 10 years earlier with half the annual contribution produces better results.

Traditional vs. Roth: The Core Decision

The primary choice in retirement account type is between traditional (pre-tax contributions, taxed on withdrawal) and Roth (after-tax contributions, tax-free withdrawal). The financial logic of the choice: if you expect to be in a higher tax bracket in retirement than you are today, Roth is better — you pay taxes now at the lower rate. If you expect to be in a lower tax bracket in retirement, traditional is better — you defer taxes to when they will be lower.

For most people early in their careers — who are in relatively low tax brackets and have decades for tax-free Roth growth to compound — Roth accounts are strongly advantageous. As income rises and tax brackets increase, traditional (pre-tax) contributions become more valuable. Many financial planners recommend maintaining both types to create "tax diversification" in retirement — the ability to draw from either source depending on annual tax circumstances.

401(k) and Employer Matching

If your employer offers a 401(k) match, contributing enough to capture the full match is the highest-return investment available — it is an immediate 50–100% return on your contribution (depending on the match formula), before any market returns. Leaving employer match on the table is equivalent to turning down part of your salary. This contribution should be made before any other investment, debt paydown above minimums, or savings.

The Retirement Account Priority Ladder

Once a starter emergency fund is in place, the optimal order for allocating investment dollars is: (1) 401(k) up to the employer match, (2) Pay off high-interest debt (above ~7% APR), (3) Roth IRA up to the annual contribution limit, (4) 401(k) up to the annual contribution limit, (5) Taxable brokerage account for additional investments. This order maximizes the value of tax advantages and guaranteed returns while maintaining appropriate debt management. Chapter 10 sets it out in full, including where the emergency fund belongs.

Social Security: What You Need to Know

Social Security is a foundational component of most Americans' retirement income, yet it is widely misunderstood. Key facts: Social Security benefits are based on your 35 highest-earning years; if you have fewer than 35 years of covered earnings, zeros are averaged in; your benefit amount is determined by claiming age, with benefits increasing approximately 8% for each year you delay claiming between 62 and 70.

The claiming age decision is one of the most significant financial decisions in retirement: claiming at 62 (the earliest eligible age) locks in a permanently reduced benefit; claiming at 70 maximizes the lifetime benefit for those who live to average or above-average life expectancy. For married couples, coordinating Social Security claiming strategies can significantly increase lifetime household benefits — a topic worth consulting a fee-only financial planner about as you approach retirement age.

The Roth Conversion Strategy

A Roth conversion involves moving money from a traditional IRA or 401(k) to a Roth IRA, paying income tax on the converted amount in the year of conversion. For people who expect to be in higher tax brackets in retirement than they are currently — either due to rising income or expected changes in tax law — strategic Roth conversions during lower-income years can significantly reduce lifetime tax liability. This strategy is particularly relevant for early retirees with income gaps before Social Security or pension income begins.

IRA Contribution Limits and Eligibility

IRA (Individual Retirement Account) contribution limits are set by the IRS and adjusted periodically for inflation. For 2026 the annual contribution limit is $7,500 ($8,600 for those 50 and older). Roth IRA eligibility phases out at higher income levels — check the current IRS income limits before contributing. If your income exceeds Roth IRA eligibility, the "backdoor Roth IRA" — a legal strategy involving a non-deductible traditional IRA contribution followed by a Roth conversion — may be available to you.

The Self-Employed Advantage

Self-employed individuals and business owners have access to retirement accounts with significantly higher contribution limits than employees: the SEP-IRA allows contributions up to 25% of net self-employment income (up to a substantial annual cap); the Solo 401(k) allows both employee and employer contributions up to an even higher combined limit. These accounts represent one of the most valuable financial tools available to self-employed individuals and are significantly underutilized.

The FIRE Movement: Financial Independence, Retire Early

The FIRE (Financial Independence, Retire Early) movement has brought mainstream attention to an approach to financial planning that prioritizes accumulating enough invested assets to cover living expenses without employment income — financial independence — rather than working to a traditional retirement age. The core math: if you can live on 4% of a portfolio annually (the "4% rule"), you need 25x your annual expenses saved to be financially independent.

FIRE practitioners typically achieve financial independence through: extremely high savings rates (40–70% of income rather than the conventional 15–20%), aggressive expense reduction focused on the big three (housing, transportation, food), and optimized investment strategies using index funds.

The approach requires significant sacrifice during the accumulation phase but produces the option of complete work-optional freedom years or decades earlier than conventional retirement planning.

Which FIRE Variant Fits Your Life

FIRE has several variants that accommodate different income levels and lifestyle preferences. Lean FIRE targets financial independence with minimal annual expenses (often under $30,000/year). Fat FIRE targets financial independence with higher annual expenses, requiring a larger portfolio but providing a more comfortable lifestyle. Barista FIRE targets partial financial independence — enough invested assets to reduce work to part-time, with some continued income covering remaining expenses. Each variant requires different accumulation targets and timelines.

Choosing When to Claim Social Security

Delaying Social Security claiming from age 62 to age 70 increases monthly benefits by approximately 76%. For someone with a normal life expectancy and no urgent financial need for early benefits, delayed claiming produces a substantially higher lifetime income. The break-even analysis — the age at which delayed claiming produces more total income than early claiming — typically falls between 78 and 82 years. Given that average life expectancy for 65-year-olds is approximately 85 years for women and 83 for men, delayed claiming is advantageous for the majority of people who can afford to wait. Running your specific numbers through the Social Security Administration's claiming calculator is a 30-minute investment that can produce tens of thousands of dollars in additional lifetime benefits.

Healthcare in Retirement: The Overlooked Variable

Healthcare costs are among the most significant and least adequately planned variables in retirement finance. Fidelity's 2026 estimate puts the figure at about $185,500 in today's dollars for a single 65-year-old, and roughly $371,000 for a couple retiring at the same age (excluding long-term care). This figure exceeds the total retirement savings of most Americans, yet it is rarely incorporated into retirement planning in a serious way.

Planning for healthcare costs in retirement requires understanding the gap between when employer-sponsored insurance typically ends (retirement, usually before 65) and when Medicare begins (65), the costs and coverage structure of Medicare supplements, and the potential need for long-term care coverage. Health Savings Accounts (HSAs) are uniquely valuable in this context: contributions are tax-deductible, growth is tax-free, and withdrawals for qualified medical expenses are tax-free. An HSA that accumulates throughout a working career and is invested rather than spent on current medical costs can provide a significant dedicated healthcare fund for retirement.

Roth or Traditional When the Answer Is Not Obvious

The Roth-versus-traditional rule resolves cleanly only when you have a firm expectation about your future tax bracket. Often you do not. If retirement looks likely to put you in roughly the same bracket as today, the tax arithmetic is close to a wash, and the decision turns on secondary factors instead.

Two of those factors carry the most weight. Roth accounts have no required minimum distributions, so the balance can stay invested and growing tax-free for as long as you choose. And for people in peak earning years in high tax brackets who expect their retirement spending to be significantly lower than their current income, traditional accounts that defer taxes from high-rate years to lower-rate retirement years often produce better after-tax outcomes. Where the uncertainty is genuine and neither case is clear, the most common recommendation is to split contributions between Roth and traditional — hedging against future tax rates rather than betting on them.

The Compound Interest Table: Your Most Powerful Financial Visualization

The compound interest table is the most powerful tool for visualizing the long-term impact of consistent saving and investing. A $500 monthly contribution to a tax-advantaged account earning 7% average annual returns produces approximately $605,000 over 30 years and approximately $1.3 million over 40 years. More than doubling the total between years 30 and

40 — with the same $500 monthly contribution — illustrates the exponential nature of compound growth and explains why starting early is the single most powerful variable in long-term wealth building.

The same table illustrates the cost of delay. Starting retirement saving at 25 versus 35, with the same contribution and the same return, produces a 35-year-old's portfolio worth less than half the 25-year-old's portfolio at age 65. The 10 years of contributions are only part of the difference — the compounding on those early contributions accounts for the majority of the gap. Understanding compound interest viscerally, not just mathematically, is one of the most motivating financial insights available. Run the numbers for your specific situation using any online compound interest calculator and let the results motivate consistent early saving.

Chapter 7 Exercise: Maximize Your Retirement Account Contributions

Calculate how much you are currently contributing to retirement accounts. If you have an employer match available and are not capturing the full match, increase your 401(k) contribution to capture it immediately. Check whether you are eligible for and have maximized your Roth IRA contribution for the current year. Calculate what contribution increase you would need to reach the full annual limits, and create a plan to get there.

Chapter Key Takeaways

- Tax-advantaged retirement accounts provide legal wealth building subsidies that compound dramatically over long time horizons
- Roth accounts are generally better for people early in careers; traditional accounts become more valuable as income and tax brackets rise
- Always contribute at least enough to your 401(k) to capture the full employer match — it is an immediate 50–100% return
- The priority ladder: 401(k) to match, high-interest debt, Roth IRA, 401(k) to limit, taxable accounts
- Self-employed individuals have access to SEP-IRAs and Solo 401(k)s with significantly higher contribution limits than employee accounts

Notes — Chapter 7

CHAPTER 8

Protecting What You Build: Insurance and Estate Planning Basics

---

Building wealth without protecting it is like filling a bathtub with the drain open. Insurance and estate planning close the drain.

Insurance is the one product you need but hope you never have to use.

Building wealth and protecting it are two sides of the same financial coin. The discipline that goes into accumulating assets can be undone in an instant by an uninsured catastrophe. This chapter covers the insurance and estate planning basics that every financially responsible adult needs — not as theoretical knowledge, but as concrete actions to take.

Insurance is an uncomfortable topic for most people — it involves thinking about unpleasant possibilities (illness, disability, death) and spending money on something you hope never to use. This discomfort causes chronic underinsurance, which is one of the most common causes of severe financial setbacks. A single uninsured medical catastrophe, disability event, or death of the primary earner can undo decades of disciplined wealth building.

Financial Protection from Legal Liability

One of the most overlooked categories of financial protection is liability — the risk that you could be held legally and financially responsible for harm that occurs to others. Automobile accidents, household injuries, professional errors, and even social media posts can create legal liability that threatens your financial assets.

Umbrella insurance — a policy that provides additional liability coverage above and beyond your homeowner's or auto insurance limits — is one of the highest-value, lowest-cost insurance products available. Annual premiums for $1–2 million in additional liability coverage typically cost $200–$300/year. This modest cost provides protection against the relatively rare but financially catastrophic liability judgment that could otherwise devastate a lifetime of wealth building.

Health Insurance: Non-Negotiable

Health insurance is the most important insurance product most people will ever own. Medical costs are among the most commonly cited contributors to personal bankruptcy in the United States, though researchers disagree sharply about how large a share they explain. What is not in dispute is the exposure: for someone uninsured, a single hospitalization regularly generates bills exceeding $30,000–$100,000. If employer-sponsored health insurance is available to you, enroll in it even if the premium seems high. If not, use the ACA marketplace to find coverage — subsidies are available at a range of income levels.

Understanding your health insurance is as important as having it: know your deductible (what you pay before insurance covers costs), your out-of-pocket maximum (the most you can pay in a year), your network (which providers are covered at in-network rates), and how to use your HSA (Health Savings Account) if you have a high-deductible plan — HSAs offer triple tax advantages and can function as a secondary retirement account.

Disability Insurance: Protecting Your Income

Disability insurance — income replacement coverage if you become unable to work due to illness or injury — is dramatically undervalued and underutilized. Statistics suggest that one in four working adults will experience a disability lasting longer than three months during their career. Yet most working adults carry no disability insurance beyond what their employer provides (typically 60% of salary through short-term and long-term disability plans).

For high earners whose income significantly exceeds their employer disability coverage, supplemental disability insurance is worth serious consideration. Look for: own-occupation coverage (pays if you can't perform your specific occupation, not just any occupation), benefit period to age 65, and an elimination period (the waiting period before benefits begin, typically 90 days) that you can bridge with your emergency fund.

The Insurance Audit

Once per year, audit all of your insurance coverage: health, auto, home/renters, life, disability. For each policy, confirm: Is the coverage amount still appropriate for your current situation? Have circumstances changed (new assets, new family members, changes in income) that require adjusting coverage? Are you carrying coverage you no longer need? Are you underinsured in any category?

Understanding Your Benefits Package

For employees, the annual benefits enrollment period is one of the most financially significant weeks of the year — and one of the most underappreciated. Employer-provided benefits represent substantial additional compensation: health insurance alone typically has a market value of $15,000–$25,000 annually for a family. Yet most employees make benefits elections quickly and without careful evaluation.

Key decisions worth careful annual evaluation: health insurance plan selection (HDHP vs. PPO tradeoffs, HSA contribution strategy if HDHP is selected), life insurance elections, disability coverage elections, flexible spending accounts, and any supplemental insurance options. The difference between optimal and suboptimal benefits elections can easily total several thousand dollars annually — comparable to a modest raise.

The HSA as a Retirement Account

Health Savings Accounts (HSAs), available to people enrolled in high-deductible health plans, offer a unique triple tax advantage: contributions are pre-tax, growth is tax-free, and withdrawals for qualified medical expenses are tax-free. If you can afford to pay current medical expenses out of pocket and invest your HSA contributions, the account effectively functions as a secondary retirement account — money can be withdrawn for any purpose after age 65 (paying ordinary income tax, like a traditional IRA), making it one of the most tax-efficient savings vehicles available.

Life Insurance: Who Needs It and What Kind

Life insurance is appropriate if other people depend on your income — a spouse, children, or other dependents. If you have no dependents, you likely don't need life insurance. If you have dependents, the appropriate coverage is typically 10–12x your annual income for term life insurance — pure death benefit coverage for a defined period (10, 20, or 30 years), with no investment component.

Whole life, universal life, and other permanent life insurance products are sold aggressively but are appropriate for very few individual situations. The combination of high premiums, low early cash values, and complex terms makes them poor choices for most people who need life insurance. Buy term life insurance and invest the premium difference — this approach almost always produces better financial outcomes.

Protecting Your Identity and Financial Accounts

Financial fraud and identity theft cost Americans billions of dollars annually and can cause severe, lasting damage to credit scores and financial accounts. Basic protective practices: a credit freeze at all three bureaus (free, prevents new accounts from being opened in your name, can be lifted when you need new credit), strong unique passwords for all financial accounts with a password manager, and two-factor authentication on every financial account that offers it.

Monitoring practices: review all financial account statements monthly for unauthorized transactions; check your credit report annually (or quarterly using free monitoring services); and set up transaction alerts on all bank and credit card accounts so that any charge immediately generates a notification. Early detection is the most effective response to fraud — the sooner unauthorized activity is caught, the easier it is to reverse.

How Much Coverage, and for How Long

Life insurance is not an investment — it is risk transfer. The primary question is not whether life insurance is a good investment (it is not designed to be) but whether you have dependents who would face financial hardship if your income were no longer available. For people with dependents and an income that supports them, term life insurance — which provides a death benefit for a specified term at a fixed premium — is the appropriate product for most situations. For people without dependents, life insurance may not be necessary at all.

The common rule of thumb — 10 to 12 times your annual income in coverage — is a reasonable starting point but should be adjusted for your specific situation. Higher coverage may be appropriate if you have significant debt, non-working spouses, special needs dependents, or mortgages that would require substantial insurance proceeds to pay off. Lower coverage may be appropriate if you have significant assets, both partners have income, or your dependents are nearly financially independent. A fee-only financial planner can help you calculate the appropriate coverage for your specific situation without the conflict of interest that commission-based insurance agents have.

Estate Planning Basics: The Three Documents Everyone Needs

Estate planning is often treated as a task for wealthy or elderly people. It is neither. Anyone with assets, dependents, or preferences about medical care should have three foundational documents: a will (specifying how assets should be distributed and who should care for minor children), a healthcare proxy or medical power of attorney (naming someone to make medical decisions if you are incapacitated), and a durable financial power of attorney (naming someone to manage your financial affairs if you are unable to). These three documents, prepared by an estate planning attorney for $500–$1,500, prevent the costly and emotionally painful situations that arise when people die or become incapacitated without them.

Beneficiary Designations: The Most Neglected Estate Planning Step

Beneficiary designations on retirement accounts and life insurance policies override your will. If your IRA names an ex-spouse as beneficiary and your will names your current spouse, your ex-spouse receives the IRA. This mismatch is surprisingly common and produces outcomes that are directly contrary to the deceased person's intentions. Reviewing beneficiary designations on all financial accounts — particularly after major life events such as marriage, divorce, the birth of children, or the death of a named beneficiary — is an essential financial maintenance task.

The review process is simple: contact each financial institution where you have retirement accounts, life insurance, or other accounts with beneficiary options, and request to see your current designations. Update any that do not reflect your current intentions. Add contingent beneficiaries (secondary beneficiaries who receive assets if the primary beneficiary predeceases you) to all accounts. This review takes an afternoon and prevents one of the most common and costly estate planning failures.

Digital Estate Planning: The Modern Necessity

Digital assets — online accounts, cryptocurrency holdings, digital photos and documents, intellectual property stored in cloud services, online business assets — are an increasingly significant component of personal estates that traditional estate planning documents often do not address adequately. Without explicit digital estate planning, the passwords, accounts, and digital assets that a person has accumulated over a lifetime may be inaccessible to their family after death or incapacity.

A practical digital estate plan includes: a secure password manager that a trusted person can access (including instructions for access), a digital asset inventory listing all significant online accounts and digital holdings, explicit instructions for each account (whether to memorialize, close, or transfer), and any specific wishes regarding digital content. This information, updated annually and accessible to your executor or a trusted family member, prevents the frustrating and emotionally costly process of trying to access digital assets without credentials during an already difficult time.

Chapter 8 Exercise: Your Insurance and Estate Planning Audit

Review your current insurance coverage in each category: health, disability, life, auto, and home/renters. Identify any gaps — particularly disability and life insurance if you have dependents. If you don't have a will, healthcare proxy, and power of attorney, create or schedule an appointment to create them. These documents are not expensive and are essential.

Chapter Key Takeaways

- Health insurance is the most critical insurance product — an uninsured medical catastrophe is one of the fastest routes to financial ruin
- Disability insurance protects your income against the one-in-four chance of a career-interrupting disability
- Term life insurance is appropriate and sufficient for most people with dependents — avoid whole life and universal life products
- Every adult needs a will, healthcare proxy, and power of attorney regardless of wealth level
- Annual insurance audits ensure coverage remains appropriate as circumstances change

Notes — Chapter 8

CHAPTER 9

Earning More: Raising Your Income Ceiling

Spending less has a floor; earning more has no ceiling. Both sides of the financial equation matter.

Your income ceiling is determined by the value you create for others.

Frugality is a virtue and a necessary component of financial health. But it has a floor — there is only so much you can cut before you are sacrificing genuine quality of life. Income growth has no floor and no ceiling. Both sides of the financial equation matter, and for many people, focusing exclusively on the spending side while neglecting income growth is the most costly financial oversight they make.

Most personal finance advice focuses almost exclusively on the spending side of the financial equation: cut this, eliminate that, optimize the other thing. This focus is not misplaced — spending discipline is fundamental — but it is incomplete. For people whose income is the binding constraint on their financial progress, spending optimization produces diminishing returns while income growth can produce transformational results.

Geographic Arbitrage and Remote Work

The growth of remote work has created an income optimization opportunity that simply didn't exist a decade ago: geographic arbitrage — earning income calibrated to a high-cost market while living in a lower-cost location. A software engineer earning a San Francisco salary while living in a mid-size Midwestern city can achieve savings rates and wealth accumulation timelines that would be impossible in either location independently — the high income without the high costs.

Geographic arbitrage at its most extreme involves international relocation to significantly lower cost-of-living countries while maintaining remote work income in high-wage markets. This approach, common in the FIRE community and increasingly accessible as remote work infrastructure matures, can produce extraordinary financial outcomes for people willing to embrace the lifestyle tradeoffs of expatriate living.

The Income Equation

Income can be increased through four primary mechanisms: earning more in your primary career (raises, promotions, job changes), developing and monetizing secondary skills (freelancing, consulting, part-time work), creating passive income streams (rental properties, digital products, licensing), and optimizing existing income through tax efficiency (maximizing pre-tax retirement contributions, tax-loss harvesting, business structure for self-employed individuals).

Negotiating Salary: The Most Underutilized Income Lever

Research consistently shows that salary negotiation is the highest-return time investment available to most employees. Linda Babcock's research at Carnegie Mellon found that failing to negotiate a first salary can cost an individual more than $500,000 by age 60 in foregone earnings (due to the compounding effect of higher base salary on all subsequent raises and job offers). Yet a majority of workers never negotiate salary.

Effective salary negotiation requires: researching market rates for your role using sites like Glassdoor, LinkedIn, and Levels.fyi; framing the negotiation around market data rather than personal need; targeting a specific number rather than a range (research shows that the first specific number anchors the negotiation); and being willing to ask for benefits, title, and equity when base salary has limited flexibility.

The Annual Raise Strategy

Rather than waiting for your employer to offer a raise, proactively manage your compensation annually. Three months before your performance review, document your accomplishments with specific outcomes and financial impacts. One month before your review, research current market rates for your role. In your review, make the case for a specific number based on your documented value and market data. This systematic approach produces meaningfully better compensation outcomes than passive waiting.

Building Wealth Through Business Ownership

Small business ownership and self-employment are among the most powerful paths to significant wealth creation available. The wealth-building advantages of business ownership: income potential uncapped by salary bands, equity value that can be realized through business sale, access to more favorable tax treatment, and the ability to build an asset that has value beyond your personal labor.

The risks are real and should be evaluated honestly: business failure rates are high, income is often irregular especially in early years, and the time investment required significantly exceeds typical employment. But for people with marketable skills, entrepreneurial temperament, and adequate financial reserves to bridge the startup period, business ownership can produce financial outcomes that employment cannot match.

Passive Income: Realistic Expectations

"Passive income" is one of the most heavily marketed concepts in personal finance — and one of the most misleadingly presented. Truly passive income requires either significant capital investment (dividend portfolios, rental properties) or significant upfront labor to create a durable asset (writing a book, building a course, creating software). The "passive" in passive income refers to ongoing income after initial investment or creation — not to income generated without any investment of time or money.

Realistic passive income paths for individuals without large capital: digital products (ebooks, courses, templates) that require substantial upfront creation time but generate ongoing royalties; dividend-paying index funds that require capital investment but minimal ongoing management; and rental real estate that requires both capital and ongoing management despite the "passive" categorization it often receives.

Building Income-Generating Skills

The most reliable path to higher income over a career is building skills that are both valuable (highly sought by employers or clients) and relatively scarce (not easily replaced by automation or offshore labor). Technical skills in high-demand areas, specialized domain expertise, and complex communication and leadership skills all have these characteristics. Investing deliberately in skill development — through courses, certifications, mentorship, and deliberate practice — produces compounding income returns over a career that dwarf the returns from any single financial optimization.

Side Income and the Gig Economy

Developing income outside of primary employment has been made significantly more accessible by digital platforms, remote work infrastructure, and the growth of the gig economy. The most accessible high-value side income paths: freelancing existing professional skills (writing, design, programming, consulting, teaching), selling digital products (courses, templates, guides, software), and platform-based service work (tutoring, coaching, consulting via platforms like Upwork or Coach.me).

Tax Optimization: The Deductions and Accounts Most People Miss

Tax optimization — legally minimizing your tax liability through available deductions, credits, and account strategies — is one of the highest-return financial activities available. The average American pays 20–30% of income in federal, state, and local taxes combined. Even modest optimization can produce thousands of dollars annually in tax savings.

The most impactful tax optimization strategies for most individuals: maximizing pre-tax retirement account contributions (every dollar reduces taxable income dollar for dollar), using an HSA if eligible (triple tax advantage), harvesting investment losses to offset gains in taxable accounts, and understanding which deductions you may qualify for (home office, education expenses, charitable contributions, student loan interest). None of these strategies require expensive tax professionals — they require basic understanding and consistent implementation.

The Lifetime Financial Plan

Financial planning is not a one-time event — it is an evolving process that requires updating as your life changes. The major financial planning milestones that typically require professional guidance or significant plan revision: first "real job" (benefits enrollment, emergency fund, retirement account initiation), marriage (combining finances, insurance review, estate planning), first home purchase (mortgage optimization, property tax, maintenance reserves), children (education savings, life insurance review, will update), major income changes, approaching retirement (Social Security claiming strategy, Medicare, distribution planning), and estate planning at any age.

Building Multiple Income Streams

The financially resilient life has more than one income source. Not because any one income is inadequate, but because reliance on a single income stream creates a fragility that no amount of saving can fully address. The loss of a job, a health crisis, an industry disruption — any of these can eliminate a single income source. People with multiple income streams experience the same disruptions as reduced challenges rather than existential financial threats.

The most accessible secondary income streams for most people: building skills that translate to consulting or freelance work in your primary field (which can generate income in periods of employment disruption), developing digital products that provide passive income, building investment income through consistent long-term investment (dividends and capital appreciation), and developing marketable skills in adjacent fields. The goal is not to work multiple jobs simultaneously but to build the capability to generate income through multiple channels, such that no single channel's disruption creates a crisis.

The Path From Financial Stability to Financial Freedom

Financial stability — having adequate income, manageable debt, emergency savings, and a functioning budget — is the prerequisite for financial freedom, not the destination. Financial freedom is the state in which your investment income, or the combination of investment income and reduced expenses, covers your living costs without requiring your continued active employment. This state, variously called financial independence, the crossover point, or FIRE (Financial Independence, Retire Early), is achievable at a wide range of income levels for people who pursue it deliberately.

The path from stability to freedom has two variables: the savings rate (how much you save and invest) and the investment return (what your investments earn over time). The first variable is fully within your control; the second is partially within your control (through asset allocation) and partially determined by market conditions. The mathematics of financial independence are well-established: saving 25 times your annual expenses typically provides a portfolio that has historically sustained 4% annual withdrawals for at least 30 years. Getting to 25x expenses faster requires either higher savings rates, higher income, lower expenses, or some combination. Each percentage point increase in your savings rate reduces the time to financial freedom in a nonlinear way because of the dual effect on both the accumulation rate and the expenses the portfolio needs to cover.

Chapter 9 Exercise: Your Income Growth Plan

Identify two income growth levers available to you in the next 12 months: one within your primary career (raise negotiation, promotion path, or job change), and one outside it (skill development with income application, side income opportunity, or passive income creation). Write a specific next action for each. Income growth, like wealth building, requires deliberate action — it doesn't happen by default.

Chapter Key Takeaways

- Income growth compounds: higher base salary produces higher raises, better job offers, and higher lifetime earnings
- Salary negotiation is the highest-return time investment for most employees — the majority of workers never negotiate
- Valuable, scarce skills produce the most reliable long-term income growth — invest deliberately in skill development
- Side income is more accessible than ever through digital platforms and remote work infrastructure
- Both income growth and spending discipline matter — optimizing only one side of the financial equation produces limited results

Notes — Chapter 9

CHAPTER 10

The Complete Financial Life: Putting It All Together

How the pieces of personal finance connect into a coherent system — and how to prioritize when you can't do everything at once.

The secret to getting ahead is getting started. The secret of getting started is breaking your complex overwhelming tasks into small manageable tasks, and then starting on the first one.

Personal finance advice is often delivered as a collection of individual directives: pay off debt, build an emergency fund, max out your 401(k), invest in index funds, buy life insurance, write a will. Each directive is valid. The problem is that people with limited financial resources cannot do all of these things simultaneously, and the advice rarely provides a clear priority order for doing them sequentially. The result is decision paralysis, or an attempt to do everything at half-effort that produces inadequate progress on all fronts.

This chapter provides the priority sequence — the order in which to address your financial life when resources are limited and everything seems urgent. It is not the only valid sequence; personal circumstances create legitimate variations. But it reflects the order that produces the best financial outcomes for most people across most situations, accounting for the interaction effects between different financial goals.

The Financial Priority Ladder

The financial priority ladder is the sequence of actions that produces the best expected financial outcome given a limited monthly savings amount. It is a prioritization framework, not a rigid prescription — circumstances can justify departing from it. But it provides a clear default when you are unsure which financial goal to address next.

Step 1 — Get the employer 401(k) match: If your employer matches 401(k) contributions up to a percentage of your salary, contribute at least enough to capture the full match before anything else. An employer match is an immediate 50–100% return on your contribution — no other financial action produces this guaranteed return.

Step 2 — Build a starter emergency fund: Before paying down debt aggressively or investing beyond the match, accumulate $1,000–$2,000 in a liquid savings account. This small buffer prevents every minor financial disruption from derailing your debt payoff plan.

Step 3 — Pay off high-interest debt: Pay down all debt with interest rates above about 7% using the avalanche (highest rate first) or snowball (smallest balance first) method. High-interest debt is a guaranteed negative investment — eliminating it produces a guaranteed return equal to the interest rate.

Step 4 — Build full emergency fund: Once high-interest debt is eliminated, build your emergency fund to three to six months of essential expenses in a high-yield savings account.

Step 5 — Maximize tax-advantaged accounts: Max out HSA contributions if eligible (triple tax advantage), then maximize Roth IRA or traditional IRA contributions ($7,500 annual limit in 2026), then increase 401(k) contributions toward the annual limit.

Step 6 — Invest additional savings: Invest remaining savings in a taxable brokerage account using the same index fund approach as your retirement accounts.

When to Deviate From the Standard Priority

The standard priority ladder is optimal for most situations but should be modified in specific circumstances. If you have variable income (freelancers, commission-based workers, seasonal workers), build a larger emergency fund — 6–12 months — before addressing high-interest debt aggressively, because income disruption risk is higher. If your employer does not offer 401(k) matching, move to the emergency fund and debt payoff steps immediately before investing in retirement accounts. If you have student loans with moderate interest rates (5–7%), the priority between aggressive payoff and investment is close enough that personal preference can guide the decision.

Life events legitimately disrupt the standard priority sequence. A planned major purchase (home, car, education) may justify temporary accumulation of savings in a high-yield account rather than additional debt payoff or investment. The birth of a child justifies reviewing insurance coverage and establishing estate planning documents before other financial priorities. A career transition that increases income significantly is an opportunity to increase savings rates dramatically before lifestyle inflation absorbs the increase. The priority ladder is a default; your life is the context in which it operates.

The Financial Life Milestones

Beyond the priority ladder, useful financial milestones provide benchmarks for assessing whether your financial life is on track relative to your age and income. These are rough guidelines, not rigid requirements, and they assume a middle-income career trajectory. They are most useful as directional indicators rather than precise targets.

By 30: One year's salary saved in retirement accounts. No high-interest consumer debt. Functional emergency fund of at least 3 months. Basic estate planning documents in place.

By 35: Two years' salary in retirement accounts. Net worth trending consistently positive. Adequate insurance coverage. Regular automatic investment contributions.

By 40: Three times salary in retirement accounts. Mortgage equity if homeowner. Income growing through career development or additional streams. Clear picture of retirement needs.

By 50: Six times salary in retirement accounts. Maximum retirement account contributions. Long-term care insurance consideration. Estate planning reviewed and updated.

By 60: Eight times salary in retirement accounts. Social Security strategy planned. Retirement income sources identified. Healthcare cost planning completed.

The Role of Professional Help

Personal finance is learnable by anyone, and this book provides the knowledge needed to manage your financial life effectively without professional assistance. That said, specific situations warrant professional guidance: tax situations with multiple income sources, self-employment income, or significant investment gains; estate planning for complex family situations or significant assets; investment decisions involving large lump sums (inheritance, business sale proceeds, insurance payouts); and financial planning for approaching retirement. In each of these situations, the cost of a fee-only financial planner — typically $200–400 per hour or a flat project fee — is almost always worth it.

The critical qualifier is fee-only: financial planners who earn commissions on the products they sell have structural incentives to recommend those products regardless of whether they serve your interests. Fee-only planners are paid by you and are legally obligated to act in your interest as fiduciaries. The National Association of Personal Financial Advisors (NAPFA) maintains a directory of fee-only fiduciary planners. For a single financial planning session with a qualified professional, the investment of $300–600 can produce decisions worth thousands to tens of thousands over time.

Tax Planning as Part of Financial Planning

Tax optimization is one of the most consistently underutilized opportunities in personal financial planning. Most people treat taxes as a fixed cost to be paid rather than a variable that can be managed through proactive choices. The primary tax optimization tools available to most individuals: maximizing contributions to tax-advantaged accounts (401k, IRA, HSA), strategic timing of income recognition and deductions, tax-loss harvesting in taxable investment accounts, Roth conversion strategies during low-income years, and structuring of business income for self-employed individuals.

A one-time session with a fee-only CPA or financial planner focused specifically on your tax situation typically identifies several hundred to several thousand dollars in annual tax savings through strategies you were not aware of or implementing. The cost of this session is almost always recovered within the first year. As your income and assets grow, the value of tax optimization grows proportionally — the same percentage reduction in tax liability on a $200,000 income saves four times as much as on a $50,000 income.

Chapter Key Takeaways

- The financial priority ladder provides a clear sequence for addressing financial goals when resources are limited
- Capturing the full employer 401(k) match before any other savings is the highest-return first step for most people with access to employer matching
- The standard priority can and should be modified for variable income, specific life events, and unusual circumstances
- Financial milestones by age provide directional benchmarks, not rigid requirements
- Fee-only fiduciary financial planners are worth engaging for complex situations — their fee is almost always recovered in better financial decisions

Notes — Chapter 10

CHAPTER 11

Money and Relationships: The Financial Conversations No One Teaches You to Have

---

Financial conflict is the leading cause of relationship stress and relationship dissolution. Understanding how to navigate money in relationships is as important as understanding money itself.

Money is the subject of more relationship conflict than any other, including sex, parenting, and in-laws. The reasons are deep: money is laden with values, power, security, and identity in ways that make financial disagreements feel like fundamental incompatibilities rather than logistical differences. A couple who disagrees about how much to save is not just disagreeing about a number — they are often expressing different beliefs about security and pleasure, different experiences of scarcity and abundance, and different visions of what a good life looks like. Understanding this depth is the starting point for productive financial conversations in relationships.

The couples who navigate financial life most successfully are not those without financial disagreements — every long-term couple has financial disagreements. They are those who have developed the communication skills and structural agreements that allow disagreements to be resolved without producing the corrosive ongoing conflict that damages relationships. These skills can be learned; they are not the product of unusually compatible financial personalities.

Combining Finances: The Options and Their Tradeoffs

Couples have three basic options for managing finances: full combination (all money goes into shared accounts and all decisions are made jointly), full separation (each partner manages their own finances and contributes to shared expenses proportionally), and a hybrid approach (shared accounts for joint expenses and goals, individual accounts for personal spending). Each approach has valid use cases and real tradeoffs.

Full combination works best when both partners are equally engaged in financial management, when incomes are similar or when the income differential is openly acknowledged and comfortable, and when both partners share similar financial values and spending patterns. Full separation works best for couples with very different financial histories, significant pre-existing assets, or very different incomes where proportional contribution feels fair. The hybrid approach works best for most couples — it provides the shared commitment to common goals while preserving financial autonomy that reduces day-to-day spending friction.

The Money Talk: Having Productive Financial Conversations

The most common reason couples avoid financial conversations is the fear that the conversation will reveal incompatibilities that are too significant to work around. This fear, while understandable, produces the worse outcome of unexamined incompatibilities that produce ongoing conflict without explicit resolution. A financially explicit relationship — one where both partners know the complete picture of shared finances, discuss financial goals regularly, and have agreed-upon processes for financial decisions — is consistently associated with better relationship outcomes and better financial outcomes.

A productive financial conversation structure for couples: begin with values rather than numbers. What does financial security feel like to each of you? What does a good financial life look like at 60? What are you each willing to give up for financial progress, and what are you unwilling to give up? The answers to these questions reveal whether apparent financial disagreements are genuine value differences or surface-level disagreements that can be resolved through better information or creative structure.

Raising Financially Capable Children

Financial literacy is not taught systematically in most schools, which means parents are the primary financial educators for most children. The financial habits and attitudes children observe and develop at home are among the strongest predictors of their adult financial behavior. Parents who want to raise financially capable children need to both model good financial behavior and teach financial concepts and skills explicitly.

The developmental approach: for children under 10, focus on the basic distinction between needs and wants, the concept of saving for specific goals, and the experience of making small financial decisions with real money (an allowance provides this opportunity). For children 10–15, introduce concepts of budgeting, the difference between earned income and passive income, and the basic mechanics of how banks and interest work. For teenagers, introduce investing concepts, the time value of money, and the practical financial skills of managing a checking account, understanding credit, and filing taxes. The goal is a young adult who enters financial independence with the practical knowledge and psychological relationship with money that most people spend years developing through costly trial and error.

Financial Recovery After Major Setbacks

Job loss, divorce, serious illness, business failure, and major unexpected expenses are financial setbacks that affect most people at some point. The financial and psychological consequences of these setbacks are real and significant. But they are not permanent unless treated as permanent. The financial recovery from major setbacks follows predictable patterns that are worth understanding before you face them.

The psychological component of financial recovery is as important as the practical one. Financial setbacks often produce shame, which produces avoidance of financial information, which produces worse decisions, which produces more shame. Breaking this cycle requires treating the setback as a circumstance to be managed rather than evidence of personal inadequacy. The practical steps — assessing the complete financial picture honestly, prioritizing the most urgent obligations, seeking professional help when needed, and building a step-by-step recovery plan — become possible once the psychological avoidance is addressed. Many people who have experienced significant financial setbacks describe the recovery as producing a more deliberate and conscious financial life than they had before the setback occurred.

Combining Financial Philosophies in Relationships

Couples rarely have identical financial philosophies, and the differences that emerge are often more fundamental than surface-level disagreements about specific purchases. One partner may prioritize security; the other may prioritize experience. One may be oriented toward the long-term future; the other toward present enjoyment. These philosophical differences are not problems to be solved but realities to be navigated through explicit conversation and structural compromise.

The structural compromise that works for most couples with different financial philosophies: agree on the shared financial goals (emergency fund target, retirement savings rate, debt payoff timeline) and automate the behaviors that advance those goals, then give each partner genuine autonomy over their personal discretionary spending. The personal spending account each partner controls eliminates the ongoing friction of divergent spending preferences while preserving shared commitment to the financial goals that require coordination. The key insight: you can have different spending philosophies and still share identical financial goals.

Chapter Key Takeaways

- Financial conflict in relationships is usually about values and identity, not just money — productive conversations address values first
- No single financial structure (combined, separate, or hybrid) is universally best for couples — the right structure depends on specific circumstances and shared values
- Financial literacy develops through age-appropriate experiences and explicit teaching — parents are the primary financial educators for most children
- Major financial setbacks are recoverable through a combination of honest assessment, prioritized action, and the psychological shift from shame to problem-solving
- Financially explicit relationships — where both partners know the full picture and discuss goals regularly — produce better relationship and financial outcomes

Notes — Chapter 11

CHAPTER 12

Building Lasting Financial Habits: The Long Game

The principles that determine whether your financial changes stick for years or fade in months.

> ***"It is not how much money you make, but how much money you keep, how hard it works for you, and how many generations you keep it for." — Robert Kiyosaki***

Financial improvement is not a project with an end date — it is a practice with a lifetime horizon. The people who achieve lasting financial transformation are not those who complete a 30-day money challenge. They are those who internalize financial principles deeply enough that good decisions become habitual — the automatic product of a well-designed system and a financial identity built over years of consistent behavior.

This chapter addresses the long game: the psychological foundations of lasting financial change, the maintenance systems that keep financial progress on track through the inevitable disruptions of real life, and the mindset shifts that distinguish people who achieve genuine financial freedom from those who perpetually chase it.

The Habit Architecture of Financial Success

Research on the financial behavior of high net worth individuals consistently identifies a small set of behavioral patterns distinguishing them from peers with similar incomes. They automate savings before spending decisions are made. They review their financial situation regularly rather than reactively. They have clear written financial goals updated annually. They make investment decisions from a plan rather than from market news. And they consistently prioritize savings rate over consumption rate.

None of these behaviors requires unusual intelligence, discipline, or luck. They are habits — patterns practiced until they run automatically. The financial habits that seem to require extraordinary willpower in year one require almost no willpower in year five, because the neural pathways are established and the identity has shifted to accommodate them. The goal of this book is to help you build that architecture.

The Annual Financial Review

The most powerful single financial maintenance practice is the annual financial review — a dedicated two to three hour session reviewing your complete financial picture, assessing progress against goals, updating your plan, and setting targets for the coming year. This practice prevents the gradual drift that causes financially intentional people to become unintentional over time.

The annual review covers: net worth and year-over-year trend, savings rate assessment, investment allocation review and rebalancing, insurance coverage review, estate planning document review, progress toward each active financial goal, and specific targets for the coming year. This comprehensive review, done annually with genuine attention, prevents the financial blind spots that cause people to discover years of missed opportunities only when a crisis forces engagement.

Financial Setbacks as Data

Every person who reaches significant financial milestones has experienced setbacks: unemployment, accumulated debt, investment losses, expensive life transitions, or simply years of poor financial decisions before better habits were established. The difference between people who recover and those who are permanently derailed is almost entirely psychological: whether the setback is treated as information or as judgment.

The recovery mindset treats financial setbacks as data about what went wrong and what needs to change, not as evidence of fixed character. It asks: What exactly happened? What decisions contributed? What structural vulnerabilities allowed this? What changes would prevent recurrence? These questions produce actionable information. The shame-based response — avoidance and denial — produces nothing useful. The recovery plan is always the same in structure: assess honestly, prioritize urgent obligations, develop a sequential plan, implement with automated systems where possible, review monthly.

Wealth, Well-being, and What Money Actually Buys

The research on money and happiness has itself been revised, and the revision matters. Kahneman and Deaton's much-quoted 2010 finding — that emotional well-being stops improving above roughly $75,000 a year — was re-examined in a 2023 adversarial collaboration between Kahneman, Matthew Killingsworth and Barbara Mellers, which found that for most people well-being keeps rising with income well beyond $100,000, and flattens only for the least happy fifth. What survives is the practical point, and it is the one that matters here: personal finance is not primarily about maximizing wealth but about building a financial life that supports your specific well-being — adequate security, freedom from financial anxiety, the ability to pursue experiences and relationships that matter to you.

The people most satisfied with their financial lives are not the wealthiest but those whose financial behavior is aligned with their financial values — who are building toward something specific they genuinely want, making steady progress, and not sacrificing the present in ways that produce regret for an imagined future. Financial satisfaction is the product of alignment between your money and your life. This book provides the tools to build that alignment. The life it enables is yours to define.

Starting From Where You Are

The single most common financial regret is not starting sooner. The person who starts saving at 35 regrets not starting at 25. The person who starts at 45 regrets not starting at 35. This regret is natural and understandable, but it is worth examining: it assumes that the future is fixed and that the only variables are how far back the starting point was. In reality, the future is not yet written, and the starting point you have today is the only one available to you.

Whatever your current financial situation — regardless of your age, your debt level, your income, your previous financial choices — the principles in this book apply to you right now, starting from exactly where you are. The compound growth that would have been more powerful starting 10 years ago is still powerful starting today. The habits that would have been easier to establish in your 20s can still be established in your 40s or 50s. The financial life that feels impossibly distant from your current situation is being built or neglected, right now, by the financial decisions you make today. Begin.

Generational Wealth and Financial Legacy

Generational wealth is built through the same mechanisms as individual wealth, applied over longer time horizons. For most people, generational wealth is not built through inheritance of large sums but through the inheritance of financial knowledge, habits, and human capital. Children who grow up observing good financial behavior, learning financial principles, and developing a functional relationship with money are the primary recipients of generational financial advantage. The most valuable thing you can pass to the next generation is not money but the knowledge and habits that produce it.

The financial principles in this book work at any income level and at any age. The person who implements them at 25 will be in a dramatically different financial position at 65 than the person who implements them at 45 — but both will be in a dramatically better position than the person who never implements them. Start where you are, with what you have, using what you know. The mathematics of compound growth are patient; they reward anyone who begins, regardless of when the beginning happens.

Chapter 12 Exercise: Your Financial Life Vision

Write a one-page description of your ideal financial life at age 65. Be specific: what does your net worth look like? How are you spending your time? What are your income sources? What does your typical week feel like? What are you no longer worried about? Now work backward: what would you need to have accomplished by age 50 to reach that vision? By 40? By the end of this year? This backward planning exercise converts a distant aspiration into concrete near-term targets.

Chapter Key Takeaways

- Lasting financial change is built through habits and systems, not through periodic intense effort
- The annual financial review is the most important single financial maintenance practice for long-term course correction
- Financial setbacks are data about what needs to change — the recovery mindset produces specific actionable plans rather than shame-driven avoidance
- Generational wealth is built primarily through the inheritance of financial knowledge and habits, not just financial assets
- Financial satisfaction is the product of alignment between your money and your values, not the achievement of a specific wealth number

Notes — Chapter 12

CONCLUSION

Your 12-Month Money Transformation Plan

The principles in this book are not complicated. The actions required to implement them are not technically demanding. What makes personal finance hard is the intersection of psychology and consistency — the need to make good financial decisions repeatedly, over years and decades, in the face of competing desires, social pressure, and the fundamental difficulty of prioritizing future well-being over present consumption.

The 12-month plan below sequences the key actions in the order that produces the best results. Some of these actions are one-time setups. Others are recurring practices. Together, they constitute a complete personal finance system that, maintained consistently, produces financial security and long-term wealth for anyone who implements it.

Month-by-Month Action Plan

- Month 1: Calculate your financial baseline (4 numbers). Identify and name your primary money scripts. Open a high-yield savings account if you don't have one.
- Month 2: Design your spending plan. Set up automatic savings transfer. Pull your credit report and check for errors.
- Month 3: List all debts with rates and balances. Choose payoff strategy. Call your highest-rate credit card to negotiate a lower rate.
- Month 4: Open Roth IRA if eligible and not yet open. Confirm you are capturing full 401(k) employer match.
- Month 5: Audit your insurance coverage. Create will, healthcare proxy, and power of attorney if you don't have them.
- Month 6: 6-month financial review. Recalculate all 4 baseline numbers. Assess progress on debt paydown and savings rate.
- Month 7: Begin documenting accomplishments for annual review.
- Month 8: Increase automatic savings/investment transfer by 1%. Review subscriptions and cancel any unused services.
- Month 9: Review beneficiary designations on all financial accounts. Research market salary rate for your role.
- Month 10: Execute salary negotiation or promotion conversation if applicable.
- Month 11: Maximize Roth IRA contribution for the year if not yet at limit. Review investment expense ratios.
- Month 12: Annual financial review. Recalculate net worth. Set financial goals for the coming year.

Building Generational Wealth

The financial habits described in this book, practiced consistently over a lifetime, produce not just personal financial security but the potential for generational wealth — financial assets and knowledge that can be passed to your children and grandchildren. Generational wealth is not exclusively the province of the already wealthy; it can be built from any starting point through disciplined accumulation over long time horizons.

Equally important is the financial education that accompanies the assets. Research on inheritance behavior consistently finds that financial assets transferred to recipients without financial education are frequently dissipated within one to two generations — a phenomenon called "shirtsleeves to shirtsleeves in three generations" that appears across cultures and economic systems. Teaching financial principles to your children — through conversation, modeling, and age-appropriate financial responsibility — may ultimately be more valuable than the assets themselves.

The Financial Independence Mindset

Financial independence — the state in which your investment income covers your living expenses — is the ultimate goal of the financial habits described in this book. It is not merely a financial condition; it is a psychological one. The person who knows that they do not need to work for income is in a fundamentally different relationship with their employer, their time, and their choices than the person who cannot afford to stop working.

Financial independence does not require early retirement. Many financially independent people continue to work — because they enjoy their work, because it provides purpose and community, because they want to continue contributing to something beyond their own financial security. The value of financial independence is not the retirement it enables but the freedom it provides: the freedom to choose work you find meaningful, to say no to situations that compromise your values, to take career risks that would be too financially dangerous otherwise.

You do not need to be rich to be financially independent. Depending on your expected lifestyle, financial independence may require $500,000 in invested assets, or $1 million, or $2 million, or more. But the path to any of these figures is the same: spend less than you earn, invest the difference consistently in low-cost index funds, and give compound growth the time it needs to do its work. Followed patiently and consistently, this approach produces financial independence for virtually anyone who applies it.

The Long View

Financial security is not built in a month or a year. It is built across a career through the consistent application of sound principles — spending less than you earn, paying yourself first, avoiding bad debt, protecting what you build, and patiently allowing compound growth to do its work. These principles are not glamorous. They do not promise quick riches. But they work — for anyone who applies them consistently and gives them time.

FREQUENTLY ASKED QUESTIONS

What People Most Often Ask About Money

These questions represent the genuine confusions and concerns that arise most consistently when people try to take control of their finances.

I don't make enough money to save. Where do I start?

Start with $5/week. This is not a joke — it is a genuine answer to a genuine constraint. The purpose of starting with a trivially small amount is not the amount itself; it is building the habit and infrastructure of saving. Open a high-yield savings account. Set up an automatic weekly transfer of $5. Now you are someone who saves automatically. Increase the amount when you can. The habit and the account exist; the amount is simply a variable to increase over time.

Should I pay off debt or invest?

The mathematical answer: compare the guaranteed after-tax return of paying off debt (equal to the debt's interest rate) against the expected after-tax return of investing. High-interest debt (above ~7%) should be paid off aggressively before investing beyond retirement account matching. Lower-interest debt (below ~4%) should generally be maintained at minimum payments while investing, since expected investment returns exceed the debt's cost. Debt between 4 and 7% is the judgment zone — personal preference for debt freedom vs. long-term investment accumulation both have merit.

Is a financial advisor worth it?

A fee-only fiduciary financial advisor — one who charges by the hour or a flat annual fee, not commissions on products sold — is worth consulting for major financial decisions: tax-optimized retirement income planning, complex estate situations, significant inheritance, business sale proceeds, or other one-time events with large financial implications. Ongoing advisory relationships charging 1% of assets annually are harder to justify for most people with straightforward situations, since that fee compounds significantly over decades.

How do I talk about money with my partner?

Money is the most commonly cited source of relationship conflict. The most important practices: schedule a regular "money date" (monthly or quarterly) to review financial status and decisions together; establish shared financial goals that both partners have genuinely participated in setting; maintain individual spending autonomy within a mutually agreed discretionary allocation; and discuss financial decisions above a mutually agreed threshold amount before acting. Avoiding financial discussions doesn't prevent money conflicts — it guarantees them.

What do I do with a windfall?

When you receive unexpected money — a bonus, an inheritance, a tax refund, a settlement — the research suggests waiting 30 days before making any significant financial decision with it. The emotional state that accompanies windfalls produces spending decisions that cooler deliberation would modify. After 30 days, allocate the windfall following your priority ladder: high-interest debt, then the full emergency fund if it is not complete, then tax-advantaged contributions, then additional investment. The temptation to treat windfall money as "extra" and spend it on consumption is understandable — but investing it instead produces compounding benefits that far exceed the short-term pleasure of spending.

How much do I need to retire?

The most widely used estimate is 25x your expected annual retirement expenses, based on the 4% rule — the research finding that a portfolio can sustain 4% annual withdrawals for at least 30 years with high probability. If you expect to spend $50,000/year in retirement, you need approximately $1.25 million. If $80,000, approximately $2 million. These numbers are simplified — they don't account for Social Security income, which can significantly reduce the required portfolio, or for the sequence-of-returns risk that affects early retirees. But as a planning target, 25x expected annual expenses is a reliable starting point.

IMPLEMENTATION

Your 90-Day Action Plan

A clear, sequenced set of actions to implement within the next 90 days — regardless of where you are starting from.

Personal finance does not improve through knowledge alone — it improves through action. The concepts in this book are simple; the behavior changes require consistent effort over time. The following action plan is designed to convert the knowledge in this book into concrete next steps with clear timelines.

Your First 30 Days

In the first 30 days, the goal is clarity: complete, accurate knowledge of your current financial situation. Most people avoid this clarity because they fear what they will find. The fear is almost always worse than the reality, and even when it is not, knowing your situation accurately is the necessary first step toward improving it.

- Calculate your current net worth: list all assets (checking, savings, investments, property value) and all liabilities (mortgage, student loans, car loans, credit card balances). Subtract liabilities from assets.
- Track every dollar spent for two weeks without changing your spending. The goal is information, not judgment.
- Identify your three highest-interest debts and your current minimum monthly payments on each.
- Set up automatic transfers to a high-yield savings account for your starter emergency fund if you don't have one.
- Review your employer benefits to confirm you are capturing any available 401(k) match.

Days 31–60: Systems

In the second 30 days, the goal is systems: automated, sustainable financial structures that produce good outcomes without requiring constant decision-making.

- Set up your budgeting system — whether a simple spreadsheet, an app, or the envelope system — based on what you observed in your first 30-day tracking period.
- Automate your savings and investment contributions at a defined percentage of each paycheck.
- If you have high-interest debt, set up an automatic additional payment above the minimum on your highest-rate balance.
- Review your insurance coverage and identify any significant gaps.

- If you don't have a will and have dependents or significant assets, schedule an appointment with an estate planning attorney.

Days 61–90: Optimization

In the third 30 days, the goal is optimization: improving what is already working and addressing the next priority in your financial sequence.

- Review your spending data from the first 60 days and identify the one to two categories where you want to redirect spending toward your financial goals.
- Confirm your investment accounts are in low-cost index funds and your asset allocation is appropriate for your timeline.
- If your emergency fund is not yet at three months of expenses, establish a clear timeline to reach it.
- Have the money conversation with your partner if applicable — share what you have learned and align on goals.
- Set your 12-month financial goal: a specific, measurable target (e.g., "pay off $8,000 in credit card debt" or "save $5,000 in my emergency fund").

At 90 days, you will have a complete picture of your financial situation, automated systems that are improving it, and a clear trajectory. The work from that point is maintenance and progression: continuing the systems, gradually increasing savings rates as income grows, and working through the financial priority ladder until you reach financial freedom. This is the complete work of personal finance. It is not complicated. It takes time. And it absolutely works.

The Compounding Effect of Financial Knowledge

Reading this book represents a significant investment in financial knowledge. But knowledge has value only when it produces behavior change, and behavior change has value only when it is sustained over the years and decades that personal finance requires. The most important action you can take after finishing this book is a simple one: open the account, make the transfer, have the conversation, write the will. Do one specific thing today that moves you one step forward in your financial life. That one action, and the next one, and the one after that, are how the knowledge in this book becomes the financial life you are capable of building.

Return to this book annually, at your financial review. The chapter that seemed most relevant on first read may not be the most relevant in three years, when your financial situation has changed. The concepts that seemed abstract when you had no investments will be immediately practical when you do. The estate planning chapter that seemed premature in your 30s will feel urgently relevant in your 40s. This is a reference as much as a read, and its usefulness will grow as your financial life grows in complexity.

ADDITIONAL QUESTIONS

More Answers to Common Money Questions

Honest answers to the financial questions people ask most often.

These questions represent the genuine uncertainty and confusion that most people experience when managing their personal finances. They are answered with the same commitment to clarity and practicality that guides the rest of this book.

Can I pay off debt and invest at the same time?

The mathematical answer depends on interest rates: if your debt interest rate exceeds your expected investment return (roughly 6–7% for a diversified equity portfolio over the long term), pay off debt first. If your interest rate is below this threshold, investing may produce better long-term outcomes. The behavioral answer is more important for most people:

whichever approach you will stick to consistently produces better outcomes than the theoretically optimal approach you cannot sustain. Many people do both simultaneously — directing a portion of available funds to debt payoff and a portion to investment — because the psychological benefit of making progress on both simultaneously improves adherence.

How much should I have saved by my age?

The commonly cited benchmarks — one times salary saved by 30, three times by 40, and so on — are useful directional guidance but should not be treated as precise requirements. They assume continuous full-time employment from early career, average savings rates, and average investment returns. People who started investing late, took career breaks, worked in lower-paying fields, or experienced significant setbacks will have different numbers. The more important question is whether your current savings rate, if maintained, will produce adequate retirement income for your specific lifestyle. A retirement calculator that uses your specific inputs produces a more accurate and useful answer than any general benchmark.

Is it better to rent or buy a home?

This question has no universal answer because it depends on variables that are highly specific to your location, financial situation, and life plans. Buying tends to produce better financial outcomes than renting when: you plan to stay in the location for at least five to seven years, you can afford a 20% down payment without depleting emergency savings, the monthly cost of ownership (mortgage, property tax, insurance, maintenance) is comparable to or below rental costs in your market, and you are financially stable enough to absorb ownership-specific risks. Renting is often the better financial choice in expensive markets, for people with uncertain job locations, for people without significant down payment savings, or for people who cannot handle the financial risk of a major repair. The "renting is throwing money away" cliché is simply wrong — housing payments include the cost of the housing services you consume regardless of whether you own or rent.

How do I start investing if I have no experience?

Open an account at a low-cost brokerage (Fidelity, Vanguard, or Schwab are all excellent choices). If it is a retirement account, select a target-date retirement fund matching your expected retirement year — this provides instant diversification and automatic rebalancing without any ongoing decisions required. If it is a taxable account, invest in a simple three-fund portfolio: a US total market index fund, an international index fund, and a bond index fund in proportions appropriate for your age and risk tolerance. Set up automatic recurring contributions. Do not check the account value daily. Do not change your investments based on news. Let time and compound growth do the work. This simple approach outperforms the vast majority of actively managed approaches over the long term.

What is the fastest way to improve my credit score?

Credit scores respond most quickly to four interventions. First, pay down credit card balances — credit utilization (the ratio of your balance to your credit limit) is the second most important factor in your score, and reducing utilization below 30% produces rapid score improvements. Second, ensure all bills are being paid on time — payment history is the single most important factor, and any late payment significantly damages your score. Third, avoid opening new credit accounts unless necessary — each application produces a hard inquiry that temporarily reduces your score. Fourth, if you have no credit history, a secured credit card (backed by a cash deposit) can build credit history quickly when used for small purchases and paid in full monthly. Most people with damaged credit can achieve a "good" score (670+) within two to three years of consistent responsible credit use.

I'm overwhelmed by financial stress. Where do I start?

Start with the smallest, most concrete action available to you. Not the most important action — the most manageable one. Financial overwhelm is addressed by momentum, and momentum is created by completion. Open the account you have been avoiding opening. Make the call to negotiate the interest rate. Write down every debt balance on a piece of paper. These actions do not solve the problem, but they break the avoidance cycle that prevents any progress. Each small action makes the next action more accessible. Within a few weeks of consistent small actions, the overwhelming financial picture typically resolves into a manageable set of specific problems with specific solutions — which is what it actually was all along.

How do I protect myself from financial fraud and scams?

Financial fraud costs Americans tens of billions of dollars annually, and the methods are constantly evolving. The most reliable protection is a simple rule: if an investment or financial opportunity sounds too good to be true, it is. Guaranteed high returns, pressure to act immediately, unsolicited offers, requests for unusual payment methods (wire transfers to overseas accounts, gift cards, cryptocurrency), and claims that only a few people have access to this opportunity are all warning signs that should trigger immediate skepticism rather than excitement.

Practical protections: freeze your credit with all three major bureaus (Equifax, Experian, TransUnion) — this prevents new accounts from being opened in your name and costs nothing. Use a password manager with unique strong passwords for all financial accounts. Enable two-factor authentication on every financial account that offers it. Never give account information, Social Security numbers, or passwords to anyone who contacts you by phone or email, regardless of who they claim to be — call the institution directly using a number from their official website if you need to verify.

A large sum has just arrived. What are the first steps?

A financial windfall — inheritance, bonus, settlement, insurance payout, or any sudden large sum — requires a different decision framework than regular income because of its psychological uniqueness and the intensity of conflicting pressures around it. The primary recommendation: do nothing for 30 days. Deposit the money in a high-yield savings account and let the dust settle before making any significant decisions. Windfalls generate immediate pressure from every direction — family expectations, salespeople, your own enthusiasm — and the quality of decisions made under this pressure is typically worse than decisions made after calm reflection.

After 30 days, apply the windfall systematically: address any high-interest debt first, fully fund your emergency fund if it is not complete, maximize tax-advantaged account contributions for the current year, and invest the remainder in a taxable brokerage account using your standard investment approach. If the windfall is large enough to raise genuine questions about tax implications, estate planning, or investment strategy, this is the appropriate time to engage a fee-only financial planner for a single planning session. The cost of that session is typically recovered many times over in better decisions on a significant sum.

APPENDIX A

The Financial Quick-Reference Guide

Key numbers, rules of thumb, and formulas to return to again and again.

The following reference material covers the most commonly needed financial numbers and formulas. Tax limits and contribution amounts change periodically — verify current limits at IRS.gov before acting on specific numbers.

Key Rules of Thumb

- Emergency fund: 3–6 months of essential expenses in a high-yield savings account
- Savings rate target: 15–20% of take-home income; start wherever you are and increase by 1% every 90 days
- Housing: Housing costs (mortgage/rent + utilities) should ideally not exceed 28–30% of gross income

- Car: Total vehicle costs (payment + insurance + gas + maintenance) should not exceed 20% of take-home income
- Life insurance: 10–12x annual income in term life if you have dependents
- Rule of 72: Divide 72 by your expected return rate to find how many years your investment doubles
- 4% rule: You can withdraw approximately 4% of your investment portfolio annually in retirement with high probability of not running out of money over a 30-year retirement

The Financial Priority Ladder

- Step 1: 401(k) contributions up to employer match
- Step 2: $1,000 starter emergency fund
- Step 3: Pay off high-interest debt (above ~7% APR)
- Step 4: Full emergency fund (3–6 months expenses)
- Step 5: HSA to annual limit if eligible, then Roth IRA to annual contribution limit
- Step 6: 401(k) to annual contribution limit
- Step 7: Additional taxable investments

Key Financial Formulas

- Monthly savings needed to reach a goal: Goal ÷ (((1 + r)^n - 1) ÷ r), where r = monthly rate, n = months. Worked example: a $10,000 goal in 3 years (n = 36) at a 4% annual return (r = 0.04 ÷ 12 = 0.00333) gives a divisor of 38.18, so you need about $262 a month.

- Mortgage monthly payment: P × [r(1+r)^n] ÷ [(1+r)^n - 1], where P = principal, r = monthly rate, n = months
- Debt payoff timeline (minimum payments only): Use a debt payoff calculator — the math is complex but the answer is always longer than you expect
- Effective tax rate: Total taxes paid ÷ Gross income × 100
- Savings rate: (Income - Expenses) ÷ Income × 100
- FIRE number: Annual expenses × 25
- Housing cost ratio: Monthly housing costs ÷ Gross monthly income × 100 (target: below 28–30%)

Important Financial Deadlines

- Tax filing deadline: April 15 (extensions available to October 15 for filing, but not payment)
- IRA contribution deadline: April 15 of the following year — you can still contribute for last year up to that date, and a filing extension does not move it
- 401(k) contribution deadline: December 31 of the contribution year
- Quarterly estimated tax payments: April 15, June 15, September 15, January 15
- Open enrollment for employer benefits: Varies by employer, typically October-November for January coverage
- ACA marketplace open enrollment: November 1 – January 15 for the following year's coverage
- Free credit report: Available year-round at AnnualCreditReport.com; one per bureau per week

Quick Reference: Investment Account Types

401(k) and 403(b): Employer-sponsored retirement accounts with pre-tax contributions (traditional) or after-tax contributions (Roth). Annual contribution limit $24,500 in 2026 ($32,500 if 50 or older, and $35,750 for those aged 60 to 63). Always contribute at least enough to capture the full employer match. Traditional 401(k) reduces taxable income now; Roth 401(k) provides tax-free withdrawals in retirement.

Traditional IRA: Individual Retirement Account with potential pre-tax contributions depending on income and access to workplace retirement plan. Annual limit $7,500 in 2026 ($8,600 if 50 or older). Contributions may be tax-deductible. Withdrawals in retirement taxed as ordinary income. Required minimum distributions beginning at age 73.

Roth IRA: After-tax contributions with tax-free growth and withdrawals. Same annual limits as Traditional IRA. Income limits apply (phase-out begins at $153,000 for single filers in 2026). No required minimum distributions. Contributions (not earnings) can be withdrawn at any time without penalty — making it a flexible emergency reserve of last resort.

HSA (Health Savings Account): Triple tax advantage — pre-tax contributions, tax-free growth, tax-free withdrawals for qualified medical expenses. Annual limit $4,400 for individual coverage in 2026. At 65, can withdraw for any purpose (taxed as income, like a traditional IRA). Requires enrollment in a high-deductible health plan. Invest HSA funds rather than spending them for maximum long-term benefit.

Taxable Brokerage Account: No contribution limits, no tax advantages, full flexibility. Capital gains taxes apply when selling investments held more than one year at favorable long-term rates. Dividends taxed annually. Most tax-efficient for index funds held long-term. The appropriate destination for savings beyond tax-advantaged account limits.

APPENDIX B

Glossary of Financial Terms

These are the terms most commonly encountered in personal finance, defined in plain language without jargon.

- APR (Annual Percentage Rate): The yearly cost of borrowing money, including interest and fees, expressed as a percentage
- Asset allocation: The distribution of investments across asset classes (stocks, bonds, real estate, cash) in a portfolio
- Compound interest: Interest calculated on both the principal and all previously accumulated interest
- Diversification: Spreading investments across different assets, sectors, and geographies to reduce risk
- Expense ratio: The annual fee charged by an investment fund, expressed as a percentage of assets
- FICA taxes: Social Security and Medicare taxes withheld from paychecks
- Index fund: An investment fund designed to track the performance of a specific market index

- Liquidity: How quickly an asset can be converted to cash without significant loss of value
- Net worth: Total assets minus total liabilities
- Rebalancing: Periodically adjusting a portfolio back to its target asset allocation
- Vesting: The process by which an employee gains ownership of employer-contributed retirement account funds over time
- Yield: The income generated by an investment, expressed as a percentage of the investment's value

TOOLS & RESOURCES

The Best Free and Low-Cost Financial Tools

The financial tools landscape has improved dramatically over the past decade. Many of the best financial planning, tracking, and investing tools are now free or very low-cost — a stark contrast to the expensive advisory relationships that used to be required for even basic financial planning.

Budgeting and Net Worth Tracking

- Monarch Money / Copilot / YNAB: Automated expense tracking with bank account integration. YNAB charges a subscription fee but is widely considered the most effective for active budget management. Monarch and Copilot (Mac/iOS) are the closest replacements for Mint, which Intuit shut down in March 2024.
- Personal Capital (now Empower): Free net worth tracking and investment analysis tool. Particularly strong for tracking investment accounts across multiple institutions.

- Spreadsheet (Google Sheets or Excel): For people who want maximum control and simplicity, a straightforward net worth and budget spreadsheet often outperforms app-based alternatives for long-term maintenance.

Investing

- Fidelity: No minimum balance, excellent index fund lineup including zero-expense-ratio index funds, strong research tools
- Vanguard: The original low-cost index fund provider; strong for index funds and retirement accounts
- Schwab: Competitive with Fidelity; strong customer service and branch network for those who want in-person access
- M1 Finance: Excellent for automated investing with customizable portfolio "pies"; particularly good for taxable accounts

Credit Monitoring

- AnnualCreditReport.com: The only federally mandated free credit report site (one report per bureau per week)
- Credit Karma: Free continuous credit score monitoring with TransUnion and Equifax; shows credit factors and simulates changes
- Experian: Free monthly Experian FICO score with paid options for enhanced monitoring

Calculators and Planning Tools

- Investor.gov compound interest calculator: SEC-provided compound growth calculator for long-term investment projections
- Bankrate calculators: Comprehensive collection of mortgage, debt payoff, retirement, and savings calculators
- SSA.gov My Social Security: Official Social Security benefit estimate based on your actual earnings history
- FIRECalc.com: Historical Monte Carlo simulation for retirement portfolio survivability analysis

A FINAL WORD

On Getting Started

The hardest step in personal finance is the first one — not because it is technically difficult, but because it requires overcoming the inertia of avoidance, the embarrassment of facing uncomfortable numbers, and the uncertainty of not knowing exactly what to do. This book has given you a clear, sequential set of actions. All that remains is to begin.

Start today. Not next month when your schedule is less hectic, or next year when you get a raise, or after you feel more ready. Today. Pick the first action from the 12-month plan that you haven't already completed and do it now. Open the account. Make the call. Set up the transfer. The financial life you want is built one action at a time, and the first action is always the most important one because it changes the kind of person you are — from someone who intends to get their finances together to someone who is getting their finances together. That shift is everything.

The single most important financial insight that changes how people actually manage money: you cannot save your way to wealth on a low income, and you cannot spend your way to comfort on a high one. Wealth is built in the gap between income and spending, sustained consistently over time. Every financial decision you make either widens that gap or narrows it. Keeping that principle visible — returning to it regularly as your income grows and your lifestyle temptations increase — is the habit that underlies every other financial success.

Start now. With the account you can open today, the budget you can write tonight, the automatic transfer you can set up this week. The perfect financial plan that begins next year will produce less wealth than the imperfect one that begins today. Time is the one resource that cannot be recovered. Every day you delay beginning is a day of compound growth that cannot be recouped.

Money finally makes sense. Now put it to work.

YOUR MONEY JOURNAL

12 Weeks of Financial Reflection Prompts

Research on financial behavior change consistently finds that people who regularly reflect on their relationship with money — their decisions, their feelings, their progress — improve their financial outcomes faster than those who treat finance as purely a numbers exercise. The following weekly prompts support that reflection practice alongside the 90-day action plan.

- Week 1: What is my single greatest financial fear? What evidence exists that this fear is warranted? What evidence suggests it may be overblown?
- Week 2: What money scripts did I observe in my family growing up? Which have I consciously adopted? Which have I unconsciously absorbed?
- Week 3: Looking at my actual spending data: what does it reveal about what I value? What surprises me?

- Week 4: What financial decision from the past 3 months am I most proud of? What decision do I wish I had made differently?
- Week 5: If my income were to disappear tomorrow, what would I do? How does my current financial situation either support or undermine that response?
- Week 6: What is my current net worth? How does knowing this number make me feel? What is one specific thing I will do in the next 30 days to move it in the right direction?
- Week 7: What would I do with my time if money were not a constraint? What does this tell me about my relationship with work and financial independence?
- Week 8: Who are the people in my life who model the financial behaviors I aspire to? What specifically can I learn from them?
- Week 9: What financial goal am I most tempted to deprioritize right now? What would I tell a friend who was considering the same deprioritization?
- Week 10: How has my relationship with money changed since beginning this program? What beliefs have shifted? What behaviors have changed?
- Week 11: What financial legacy do I want to leave — not in terms of assets, but in terms of the financial values and practices I model for the people around me?
- Week 12: Looking back at Week 1's fear: does it still feel as large? What has changed in my financial situation and mindset over these 12 weeks?

RECOMMENDED READING

The Personal Finance Canon

These books represent the most impactful works in personal finance and behavioral economics — selected for both their evidence base and their practical applicability.

Foundational Personal Finance

- The Total Money Makeover by Dave Ramsey — Motivational debt elimination framework; best for people who need behavioral structure
- Your Money or Your Life by Vicki Robin — The original financial independence text; transformative for examining the relationship between money and time
- The Millionaire Next Door by Thomas Stanley — Research on how ordinary people actually build wealth (hint: not by looking wealthy)

- I Will Teach You to Be Rich by Ramit Sethi — Modern, practical system for automating personal finance; particularly strong for younger readers
- The Simple Path to Wealth by JL Collins — Clear, compelling case for simple index fund investing

Behavioral Finance and Psychology

- Thinking, Fast and Slow by Daniel Kahneman — The foundational text on cognitive biases and decision-making
- Misbehaving by Richard Thaler — Behavioral economics from the Nobel laureate who co-developed nudge theory
- The Psychology of Money by Morgan Housel — Excellent, readable exploration of how behavior drives financial outcomes
- Nudge by Thaler and Sunstein — How choice architecture shapes financial and other decisions

ACKNOWLEDGMENTS

A Note of Thanks

This book is for everyone who has ever felt confused, embarrassed, or overwhelmed by money — and who deserves a clear, honest explanation that doesn't require them to buy anything or trust anyone with a commission to earn.

The principles in these pages draw on decades of behavioral economics research, personal finance scholarship, and the practical wisdom of the financial independence community. The researchers and writers whose work made this synthesis possible — from Richard Thaler to JL Collins to Vicki Robin — have contributed something genuinely valuable to the world by making evidence-based financial guidance accessible outside the walls of academia and expensive advisory relationships.

Money is not the most important thing. But financial security creates the conditions in which the most important things — relationships, health, purpose, freedom — can be more fully pursued. That is why this work matters.

About the Author

Alex Z. Morgan

Alex Z. Morgan writes practical non-fiction on personal finance, side hustles, and career development. Each book translates real-world strategy into actionable frameworks readers can apply immediately. Clear Money Press publishes accessible, jargon-free guides to personal finance, investing, and wealth building.

Find our full catalog by searching Alex Z. Morgan at your preferred retailer.

Did You Enjoy Money Finally Makes Sense?

If this book helped you, I would be genuinely grateful if you took two minutes to leave an honest review. You do not need to write much — even a sentence or two makes a real difference in helping other readers find this book.

Search for the title at your preferred retailer to leave a review.

Thank you for reading. It means more than you know.

— Alex Z. Morgan

Notes

Notes

www.ingramcontent.com/pod-product-compliance
Lightning Source LLC
LaVergne TN
LVHW010722061126
851857LV00014B/1307